THE RECLAIMED WOODWORKER

21 ONE-OF-A-KIND PROJECTS TO BUILD WITH RECYCLED LUMBER

Chris Gleason

SPRING HOUSE PRESS

CONTENTS

INTRODUCTION

This book is a celebration of reclaimed wood and the beautiful range of possibilities that exist for its creative use in the home. Through the use of easy-to-follow photographs, inspired designs, and accessible building techniques, I've tried to present a comprehensive guidebook that you can use to plan and create your own furniture and other home decor projects. My interest in reclaimed wood comes directly from my twenty years of experience as a professional woodworker; while I've worked with a diverse palette of materials, my favorite projects have often involved reclaimed wood in one form or another. Why? Maybe it's because I grew up on a farm in upstate New York, and weathered, old barn wood was pretty much the backdrop for my childhood, but of course, there's more to it than that. Unlike any other material, reclaimed wood lends a sense of history and a unique, one-of-a-kind quality to any project. And, because I can source reclaimed wood nearby rather than purchasing new lumber trucked in from hundreds of miles away, using reclaimed wood allows me to live locally while pursuing some of my core values: to reduce, to reuse, and to recycle.

Still wondering if reclaimed wood is for you? If you're like most of the woodworkers I know, this important benefit should do the trick: reclaimed wood is often cheaper than traditionally sourced lumber. The key is knowing how to acquire it, so here's a short list of tips for sourcing local reclaimed lumber to get you started:

- Check your local classified ads and Craigslist.

- Ask local woodworkers where they source reclaimed wood. (I, for one, always share my sources.)

- Visit a local, independent lumber supplier; many now stock reclaimed lumber due to its popularity. If they don't, they might be able to point you in the right direction.

- Place a free or inexpensive "want" ad in the local newspaper or online.

- Offer to remove or take down an old weathered fence or shed, or place a local ad that you're willing to do so.

- Speak with a local arborist; some own small sawmills and create lumber from wood that would've otherwise been thrown away.

- Keep an eye out for old pallets. Depending on the project you have in mind, they can provide a good source of wood. (But make sure you're up to speed on the type of pallet wood to use or to avoid.)

If using reclaimed wood sounds like it might be up your alley, read on. I've provided all the details you need to build some of these great projects. Better yet, you can customize some of the details to suit your style or needs. Either way, it's thrilling to know that this book has provided some helpful guidance as you build with reclaimed lumber.

Happy building!
Chris Gleason

MIRROR FRAME

I developed this design as a project for a class. The goal was to create something really beautiful that didn't require an advanced skillset, and wouldn't take forever. As a bonus, it is a great way to use up small scraps of wood that are just too lovely to throw away. The exact result depends on the kind of material you have on hand, but also on how you decide to play your cards; there is a lot of room for creativity here. I like a nice mix of flaky paint and weathered wood tones, but however you decide to lay things out, you really can't go wrong with this one.

TOOLS

Tablesaw or jigsaw

Permanent marker

Measuring tape

Nailgun and nails

Bandsaw

Belt sander or sanding block

Clamps

Miter saw

PLAN

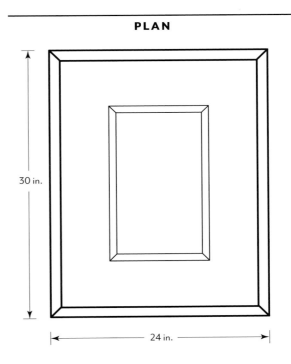

30 in.

24 in.

MATERIALS LIST

PART	QTY.	DIMENSIONS
Plywood backer	1	28 ½" x 22 ½" x ¾"
Mixed reclaimed strips		Enough to cover 6 square feet (includes extra)
Outer frame		
Long pieces	2	31" x 2 ¼" x ¾" (Before being trimmed to size)
Short pieces	2	25" x 2 ¼" x ¾"
Inner frame		
Long pieces	2	16" x 2 ¼" x ¾"
Short pieces	2	12" x 2 ¼" x ¾"
Mirror	1	18" x 12" x ¼"
Glue		
Plastic screw-on mouting clips		
Hanging hardware	1	
Finish of choice		

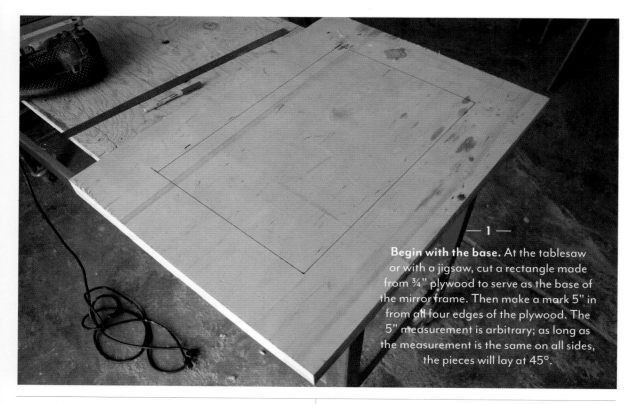

— 1 —

Begin with the base. At the tablesaw or with a jigsaw, cut a rectangle made from ¾" plywood to serve as the base of the mirror frame. Then make a mark 5" in from all four edges of the plywood. The 5" measurement is arbitrary; as long as the measurement is the same on all sides, the pieces will lay at 45°.

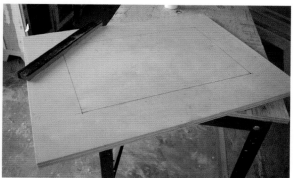

— 2 —

Overhangs are fine.
Apply glue to the first reclaimed slat and set in in place on the base. When nailing down, make sure it overhangs both the pencil lines and the outer edge of the plywood base.

— 3 —

Cover the entire rectangle—or not.
It would be easiest to simply cover the entire piece of plywood with strips that run end-to-end. However, if you find that your scraps are too short to go the distance, as long as they cross over the layout lines.

— 4 —

Position the strips. If you like, apply glue to the edges of the strips as well as the parts that contact the plywood.

— 5 —

A little goes a long way. This is a great way to use up scraps around the shop—even if you have few long strips on hand. And mix it up. Some greys, some reds, some browns . . . the wood and paint colors work well together.

— 6 —

Trim off the overhang. Using a bandsaw is a safe way to cut the outside of the frame to shape. Flipping the whole thing upside down provides a visual guide so you can see what needs to be removed.

— 7 —

Take a look. Flipping the project over, you begin to see how the roughness and variety of the stock acts as a nice counterpart to the neatly trimmed edge. Any rough edges can be smoothed with a belt sander or sanding block.

— 8 —

Prepare and saw the cutout. Flip the whole thing over again, and draw the same rectangle on the back that you did on the front. After drilling a small pilot hole for blade access, cut out the interior rectangle with a jigsaw.

— 9 —

Trim out the inside. Dress up the interior rectangle with a mitered frame that neatly fits into the opening. The mitered frame is made from stock ⅝" thicker than the mirror frame as a whole, allowing room for the mirror to attach to the back of the plywood and for picture frame-hanging hardware to be hidden.

— 10 —

Frame around the frame. Measure for the frame pieces, then cut miters on each end and test the fit. Once you have a good fit, glue and clamp each piece into place.

— 11 —

Measure it out. Work your way around the frame by lining up the miters and marking for the next corner. This approach ensures a nice, snug fit of all the parts.

— 12 —

Mark the final piece upside down. To measure the long ends of the miters, simply place the piece upside down against the mating trim pieces. When in doubt, err on the side of leaving a little extra meat on the bone and re-trimming, as needed, until you have a perfect fit.

— 13 —

Take a final look. You can apply a finish or leave the wood as-is for a more rustic appearance. The mirror is mounted from behind using small metal brackets from the hardware aisle. You can also mount the hanging device of your choice. The same design would work just as well as a picture frame, if you prefer.

PICTURE FRAME

I've been woodworking for a long time, and during that time I've made a houseful of one-of-a-kind, handmade frames. We have at least a few dozen by now. Most of them are very simple, made from scraps of whatever larger project I was working on at the time. So the frames are all unique, but each also serves as a record of work I've done. I can walk around our house and point to each frame and remember just what I was working on at that time. They're not intended as touchstones in this way, but how could they not be? Pretty cool, indeed. In this case, my wife needed a frame for her office, and I had some scraps from a bookcase that I made for a later chapter in this book. Now, every time I see the frame, I'll remember that bookcase, and probably some detail or another about what was going on when I made it.

TOOLS

Measuring tape

Miter saw

Jointer

Tablesaw

Miter gauge for tablesaw, or miter saw

Drill press or handheld drill

Pocket screw jig

Clamps

Sponge brush

PLAN

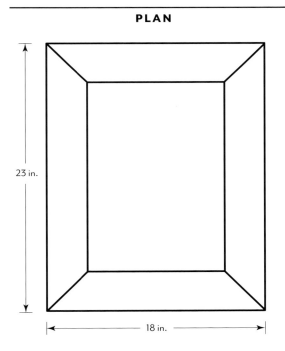

23 in.

18 in.

MATERIALS LIST

PART	QTY.	DIMENSIONS
Sides	2	23" x 2 ½" x ⅝"
Top/bottom	2	18" x 2 ½" x ⅝"
Back panel plywood blank	1	19" x 14" x ¼"
Pocket screws		1 ½"
Hanger hardware	1	¼" x 2"
Finish of choice		

— 1 —

Break down and clean up your frame stock.
If you're working from rough, old boards, begin
by cutting them down into more manageable
pieces with the miter saw. This also helps with
visualizing the layout of the pieces and working
around flaws. Use a jointer to clean up and
smooth the edges so you can make safe rip cuts
at the tablesaw.

— 2 —

Work with what you've got. The boards you
have might have some inherent limitations;
in this case, these 5"-wide boards are being
ripped into 2 ¼"-wide strips. Leave the stock a
little longer than necessary until more precise
measurements are determined.

— 3 —

Begin to cut the rabbet. Most frame
parts are rabbeted on the rear inside edge
of the stock. They're easily cut using a single
blade at the tablesaw in two passes. The
first pass is cut on the wide face of the strip, at
about half the depth of the narrow side.

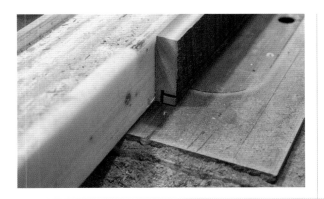

— 4 —

Living on the edge. The second pass is on the narrow edge. The two passes don't need to meet evenly, as this area won't be seen. Just don't cut so deeply that you weaken the stock.

— 5 —

Getting there. At this point, the strips have begun to resemble standard picture frame stock, but much cooler.

— 6 —

Time to start cutting the joints. Use a miter saw or miter gauge on the tablesaw to cut the first miters on one end of your frame stock. You can see now how it will shape up.

— 7 —

One corner at a time. With the strips flipped over and pressed together in the corner, put the backer board into place. Then mark the location for the corner. This "working your way around it" approach is accurate and forgiving, and it makes it easy to visualize how the frame will come to fit the object to be framed.

— 8 —

No need to reset the miter saw. You can cut opposite miters just by flipping over the workpiece instead of swinging the blade to the other side between cuts.

— 9 —

Reinforce the corners. There are several ways to reinforce frame corners; pocket screws with glue are hidden from the exterior faces of the frame. One pocket hole per corner offers plenty of strength in a frame this size. This pocket hole jig secures the work and then guides your drill bit at the correct angle for the thickness of the stock.

— 10 —

Under pressure. Fit the joint together and clamp down the workpiece to make sure nothing shifts as the screws are driven home.

— 11 —

There's always another way. Don't have or want to pull out your pocket screw jig for this one? A few brad nails through each frame piece at each corner will hold everything together.

— 12 —

Surface treatments are your choice. Flaky paint like this can be left alone, or coated with water-based polyurethane to help hold it in place.

— 13 —

Securing the artwork. Framing points are a time-honored tool for holding artwork securely in frames. They're quick and easy to set into place.

— 14 —

Hang 'er up! I added an "old standby" hanger to mount the frame. Center it on the frame and tack it in place with a few short brads or screws.

FLOATING WALL SHELF

Have you seen all the floating shelves floating around these days? Wondering how they did it? Here's one approach that is really straightforward, and pretty fun to boot. Made using recycled materials, it has an appeal that is both rustic and modern at the same time. It consists of two components—a wooden bracket that screws on the wall studs, and a five-sided box that slips onto it. Intrigued? Read on.

TOOLS

Track saw or tablesaw and jointer

Measuring tape

Clamps

Hammer

Planer

Random orbit sander

Drill press or handheld drill

Nail gun with nails

Level

PLAN

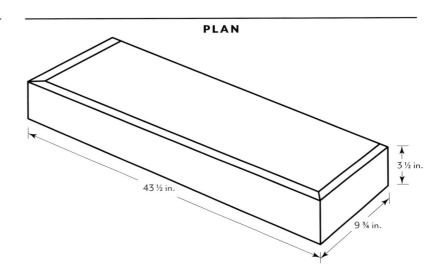

43 ½ in.

9 ¾ in.

3 ½ in.

MATERIALS LIST

PART	QTY.	DIMENSIONS	PART	QTY.	DIMENSIONS
Shelf			Bracket		
Top and bottom	2	41 ½" x 8 ¾" x 1"	Backbone	1	41 ½" x 1 ½" x ¾"
Front	1	43 ½" x 3 ½" x 1"	Arms	3	8 ¾" x 1 ½" x ¾"
Sides	2	9 ¾" x 3 ½" x 1"	Corner blocks	2	3 ½" x 3 ½" x 1 ½"
Brads		2"	Screws		#8, 3"
Glue			Screws or brads to anchor (optional)		

— 1 —

Prepare the material. You need a pair of identical panels for the top and bottom. A track saw can probably create joint-ready edges, but a tablesaw and jointer works too. The width of your stock determines how many joints you'll need. In this case, each panel required two boards. Apply glue on each edge you're joining, then clamp them together. Make sure the edges are well aligned as you apply the clamps.

— 2 —

Work on the front and sides. While the glue dries on the panels, rip some boards to width and miter their corners. This will create a more seamless look. The overall impression will be that the shelf was made from one big chunk of wood. Glue the miters and then hold them in place with some brad nails.

— 3 —

Plane the panels once the glue is dry. Skim the surface with one or two passes rather than achieve a uniformly milled surface. The goal is to enhance the character of the reclaimed wood by leaving lots of the original texture and blending in some freshly planed color and texture.

— 4 —

Stain can even out the coloration later on. If this looks like too much contrast now, you can always stain the lighter parts a bit to match the tones once the entire shelf is assembled. Even a coat of clear varnish will darken the lighter wood considerably.

— 5 —

There's a method to the madness.
Instead of sandwiching the top and bottom
panels on the edge pieces, nest them behind
the edge pieces and attach with a little glue.
This creates a uniform look across the edges,
which contributes to the monolithic feel of
the shelf. Close inspection reveals that it is a
composite of a few different pieces, but this
arrangement is preferable.

— 6 —

Brad nails hold the panels in place. Strictly
speaking, gluing and nailing the side pieces to
the top and bottom panels doesn't allow for
movement, but with a rustic piece like this, it
isn't a major concern.

— 7 —

The fully assembled box is a hollow shell.
The thickness of the parts aren't even all that
important, really. What matters is that you
have a uniform space on the inside for the
mounting bracket.

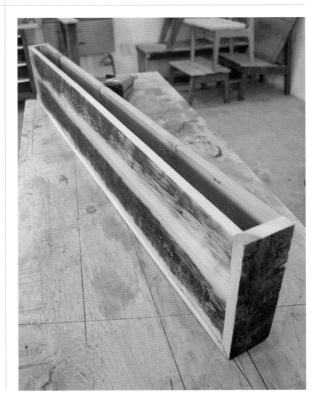

— 8 —

Time to get artistic. Because there are, by necessity, some cut edges on this piece, their color and texture need to be blended to match the character of the rest of the piece with more planing or sanding. A random orbit sander is a good tool for the job.

— 9 —

The bracket is easy to build. It is made of a backbone and three arms that stick out. The overall depth of the piece should match that of the shelf hollow.

— 10 —

Use a strong wood for the bracket. Maple is a solid choice, but oak would work just as well. To join the pieces, 3" screws provide plenty of strength, but be sure to predrill the holes to prevent splitting. Use a clamp to hold the joint together until the screw is driven home.

— 11 —

Reinforce the connections. Gluing and tacking in some corner blocks adds a lot of strength to the joint between the arms and the backbone.

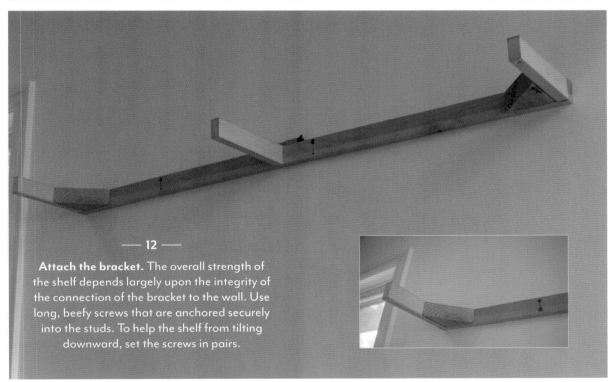

— 12 —

Attach the bracket. The overall strength of the shelf depends largely upon the integrity of the connection of the bracket to the wall. Use long, beefy screws that are anchored securely into the studs. To help the shelf from tilting downward, set the screws in pairs.

— 13 —

Pat yourself on the back. Slide the box over the bracket and you're almost done. You can anchor it with brads or small screws in an inconspicuous location. If you ever want to remove the shelf in the future, screws are preferred.

BARN DOOR

Sliding barn-style doors have been around since, well, since there've been barns. That said, they're enjoying quite a renaissance these days, and I've built and installed a ton of them. I love the look of a barn door, and part of the fun is that they can be built in such a range of styles. In this case, I found some old reclaimed wood that was a perfect fit for the rustic cabin the door was destined for.

TOOLS

Measuring tape

Tablesaw

Track saw or tablesaw and jointer

Clamps

Construction adhesive

Shims

Level

Handheld drill

MATERIALS LIST

PART	QTY.	DIMENSIONS
Door blank	1	84" x 37 ½" x ⅞"
(I glued up five 1x8s)		
Battens	5	75" x 2" x ¾"
Top and bottom rail	2	37 ½" x 4 ½" x ¾"
Glue		
Brads		1 ½"
Rail and pulley hardware set		
Hanger board	1	77" x 4" x 1"
Black ABS pipe		as needed

PLAN

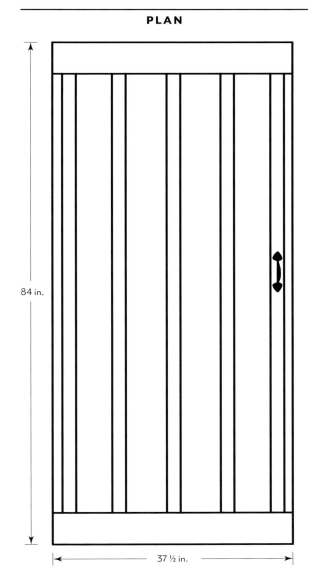

84 in.

37 ½ in.

— 1 —

Work with what you've got. Even really great materials sometimes have issues. In this case, this old barn siding must've been positioned near the ground, where it wicked up moisture over the years. The bottom 6" or so had to be cut off, but there was still plenty of good stuff left.

— 2 —

Start with straight edges. Use whatever means you have available. A track saw is a fast way to straighten one or both edges. But a jointer and tablesaw work great as well—joint one edge and then rip the other at the tablesaw.

— 3 —

Decide on the layout. Do a dry run of the glue-up, making sure you have enough stock to reach the desired width. This is also a good time to rearrange boards to determine the best-looking orientation.

— 4 —

Lay on the glue. Apply an even bead of wood glue down the full length of each board and set them in place.

— 5 —

Clamp it up. When your joints fit neatly to begin with, you don't have to rely too heavily on clamps to force the boards into place. Five clamps are more than enough to hold things in place. To help keep the panel flat, alternate clamps above and below the panel as needed.

— 6 —

Trim the door. To both reinforce the long joints between the boards and create a traditional board-and-batten look, place 2"-wide strips of a contrasting wood across the joints. Use construction adhesive and brads to secure them. You'll want to trim the top and bottom of the door with cedar 1x6s, which are attached in the same fashion.

— 7 —

Prepare to hang the door. To determine where the top of the door should be positioned, start by shimming up the bottom of the door using ½"-thick material.

— 8 —

Take a look. To get a sense for how the rail and pulleys need to be positioned, and what the relevant tolerances look like, it can be helpful to first set them up on a table. This particular hardware kit required a ¾" clearance between the bottom of the rail and the top of the door.

— 9 —

Prepare a hanger board. To support the rail, it's best to attach a 1x4 board to the wall. The rails usually come pre-drilled with holes, but they seldom line up with the studs in the wall; screwing a hanger board to the studs is an easy work around that ensures enough strength to hold the weight of the door.

— 10 —

Reinforce the connection. Construction adhesive helps ensure that the 1x4 (and the door) stay put, and prevent it from pulling away from the wall between studs.

— 11 —

On the level. A 48" level is sufficient to align the rail properly. Allow ¾" between the bottom of the board and the top of the door, as established in step **8.**

— 12 —

Shim the rail as needed. The rail may need to be shimmed out from the board at just the right distance; black ABS pipe is easy to cut to a custom length for this. (The kit included some spacers but they didn't work in this case, as the door needed to clear artwork that hung on the wall.)

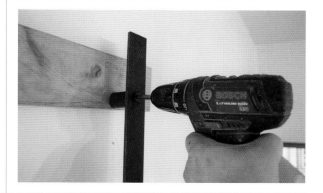

— 13 —

Hang the pulleys. With the rail attached, set the pulleys on it. This will allow you to mark the mounting holes on the front of the door.

— 14 —

Bolt it on. Drilling the door for the bolts that come with the kit is easier when the door has been pulled down. Once the holes have been drilled and the pulleys had been attached, hanging the door is a snap.

DANISH MODERN CHAIR

They say you never forget your first kiss. Well, I managed to forget mine, but I do remember the first chair that ever made me swoon: it was a curvy Danish Modern number that I found in a resale store. It was a light bulb moment, and I tried to get my hands on every book and magazine I could to learn more about the genre. This was in a pre-Internet age, so it actually took a while. Anyway, I always relish an opportunity to introduce some Danish Modern influences when I can, and this project does just that: I think the end product is fun and spunky, with a neat combination of curves and tapers. Feel free to modify the details as you like: the methods I present here are straightforward and could be applied to all kinds of other chair styles.

TOOLS

Measuring tape	Clamps
Pencil	Screwdriver
Bandsaw with ¼" blade or jigsaw	Compass or spray paint can to trace
Belt sander	Jigsaw or bandsaw
Doweling jig	Hand plane
Drill press or handheld drill or Domino	Mallet
	Stapler with staples

MATERIALS LIST

PART	QTY.	DIMENSIONS
Rear leg blanks	2	33" x 3" x 1"
Front leg blanks	2	16 ½" x 2 ½" x 1"
Side stretcher blanks	2	17 ½" x 5" x 1"
Front stretcher blank	1	16 ½" x 3" x 1"
Rear stretcher blank	1	15 ½" x 2 ½" x 1"
Seat blank (plywood)	1	22" x 17" x ¾"
Back slats	2	22" x 3 ½" x ⅝"
Glue		
Dowels		2" x ½"
Screws		#8, 3"
Wooden plugs		½" x ⅜" dia.
Screws		#8, 1 ½"
Faux sheepskin	1	24" x 24"

PLAN

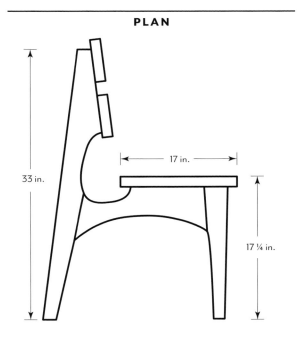

The full-size plywood mockup of the chair side is key. For more details, see the sidebar on p. 39. As a rule of thumb, the front edge of the seat should be about 17" from the floor, and it can slope down toward the back a bit.

— 1 —

Draw out the legs. Create templates from a full-size drawing and then trace the pattern onto your stock. 1" to 1 ⅛"-thick stock is nice for the legs, but you can mix it up. Just don't go thinner than ⅞". For reference, the back legs taper to 1 ¾" (front legs taper to 1 ¼").

— 2 —

Cut out the legs and stretchers. A bandsaw outfitted with a ¼" blade leaves a clean cut and can handle the sharp curves. No bandsaw? A jigsaw equipped with a stout blade is a reasonable alternative.

— 3 —

Transitions matter. The ends of the stretchers need to be absolutely flat to create a tight joint with the legs. A belt sander cleans up these spots nicely. The design of the chair side needs to allow enough width on the ends of the stretchers to accommodate the dowel joinery and a bit of extra width to provide more gluing surface.

— 16 —

Finish off the holes. Plug the holes with
⅜" wooden plugs. You can buy them pre-made
or buy a plug cutter and make them yourself.

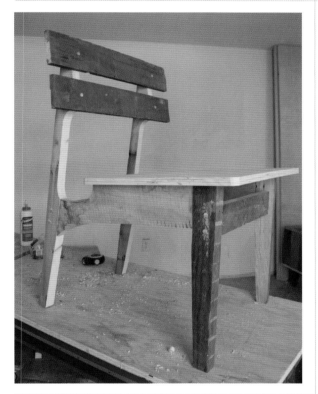

— 17 —

Fill the other holes as well. Wooden plugs
stay securely in place with just a little glue and
a few taps with a mallet.

— 18 —

Trim the slats. As the design evolves,
decide on how the ends of the back slats
should be cut. You can use paper or masking
tape to block off the waste portions to see how
it might look. Then simply cut it to shape
using a handsaw or jigsaw.

—— 19 ——

Upholstering the seat is quick and easy.
Faux sheepskin adds a fun textural contrast,
but feel free to mix it up by using the upholstery
of your choice. A small amount of material like
this is bound to be pretty inexpensive, so you
could even try a couple of different fabrics to
see which you prefer. To put on the fabric, put
some staples into the right-hand side, stretch
the fabric across toward the left until it is tight,
then staple the left-hand side. Do the same
thing on the remaining two sides. Secure the
corners last, making sure to pull in any slack so
the fabric is taut.

——20——

Attaching the seat is straightforward. Drill
countersunk holes on the bottom edge of the
side stretchers so that you can screw up into the
plywood seat blank and hold it down. This has
the advantage of providing a hidden way of
attaching the seat, and the screws will remain
accessible in case you ever want to change out
the upholstery.

— **21** —

Give it a look. The combination of the rough lumber and the sheepskin make for a decidedly modern look.

A NOTE ON DESIGN:

There are many ways to build chairs.
When I'm building chairs in a Danish Modern–inspired style, as I often do, I start by conceiving of the side of the chair as a whole. I do some sketches, which I translate into a full-size drawing. I refine the details as I go, especially in the transitions between the straight lines. When I'm satisfied with the full-sized drawing, I cut it out and trace it onto a scrap of ¼" plywood so I can cut it up and use it as a set of templates for the individual parts. To use the plywood more efficiently, you can cut out the three individual parts (rear leg, stretcher, and front leg) and trace them onto smaller scraps. You'll have less waste this way.

BENCH

The bench top is a nice place to show off some funky reclaimed wood, and the base is just unusual enough to be interesting. A miter saw, tablesaw, and drill should be pretty much all you need, and if you want to simplify the design, you could always run the boards the long way on the top instead of in a diagonal fashion like I did.

PLAN

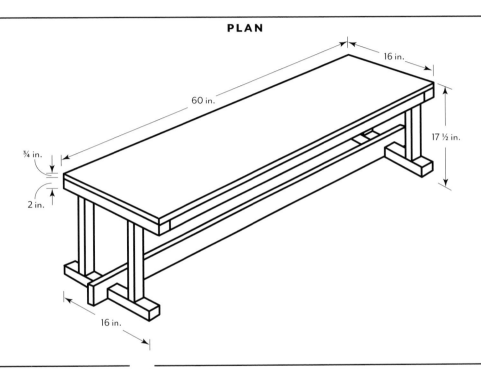

TOOLS

Tablesaw

Clamps

Pencil

Combination square

Japanese backsaw

Chisel

Straightedge

Nail gun with brad nails

MATERIALS LIST

PART	QTY.	DIMENSIONS
Legs	4	12 ¾" x 2" x 2"
Feet/base tops	4	16" x 2" x 2"
Stringers	2	56" x 4" x 2"
Screws	12	#8, 3 ½"
Stretcher	1	60" x 3" x 1"
Top	1	Enough ¾"-thick boards to cover 60" x 16"
Glue		
Construction adhesive		

— 1 —

Break down the stock. The base is made from strips that are ripped down from 2x4 lumber (in this case, they were from the era when 2x4s were actually 2" x 4").

— 2 —

Simple symmetry. The base needs two identical end assemblies. Each end of the base is made out of four parts that are glued, clamped, and screwed together.

— 3 —

Connect the assemblies. A pair of stringers made out of 2x4s connect the end assemblies. The base is shown positioned upside down, which helps keep the parts aligned during assembly.

— 4 —

Secure the stringers. A pair of 3 ½" screws at each joint offers plenty of strength to hold the assembly together and prevent racking.

— 5 —

Flip it over. To work on the bottom rail, start by flipping the assembly over. Just to mix things up, the lower stretcher is made of thinner, 1"-thick material.

— 6 —

Mark the stretcher. The stretcher needs to be notched so that it can lock into place on the lower horizontal piece of each end assembly. Use a square to ensure that the notch is laid out correctly.

— 7 —

Saw out the notch. A handsaw provides a nice, controlled way to cut out the sides of the notch. A Japanese backsaw makes quick work of it.

— 8 —

Complete the notch. A couple of chops with a chisel (running along the grain) frees up the waste. Then test the fit and fine-tune the joint as needed.

— 9 —

Attach the bottom rail. The notch fits over the mating piece and is screwed into place from below with a pair of screws.

— 10 —

Trim the edges as needed. The slats run at 15° across the seat, so cut the angle at 15° on the end of each slat. The "starter slat" needs to be trimmed so it doesn't overhang the end of the bench too far. Use a combination square to mark the location of the cut.

— 11 —

A straightedge provides a visual indicator. To help align the ends of the slats, I clamped a straightedge in place.

— 12 —

Another oddball. The slats at the ends of the bench are cut flush to the end of the bench. Once this slat is trimmed, the others fall right into place.

— 13 —

Construction adhesive to the rescue. No other adhesive is as well suited to the task; while it isn't exactly a traditional method, it sure is practical.

— 14 —

Insurance never hurts. Because the bench is made of recycled wood, seeing a few brad nails driven through the top and into the stringers doesn't hurt the aesthetic. And the extra strength never hurts.

CHAIR & STOOL COMBO

Part of the satisfaction of being a woodworker is when you want something for your home and you can jump up and say, "Yes, I can make one of those!" In this case, it was spring, which meant that my wife and I were finally able to start thinking about using our back deck again after a long winter. I started thinking about a chair, and maybe a stool to go with it; before long, I was making sketches and rummaging through my lumber supply to find just the right material. This project is the fruit of those labors, and I really like it. I also think that it could "go uptown" and live happily indoors.

MATERIALS LIST

PART	QTY.	DIMENSIONS
Chair		
Back legs	2	30" x 2" x 1½"
Front legs	2	18" x 2" x 1½"
Side stretchers	2	18½" x 3" x 1½"
Front and back stretchers	2	17" x 3" x 1½"
Seat panel*	1	22" x 18" x ¾"
Back panel*	1	22" x 24" x ¾"
Dowels		½" x ⅜" dia.
Screws		#8, 3½"
Screws		#8, 1½"
Stool		
Legs	4	17" x 2" x 1½"
Side stretchers	2	16" x 3" x 1½"
Front and back stretchers	2	17" x 3" x 1½"
Seat panel*	1	22" x 18" x ¾"
Dowels		½" x ⅜" dia.
Screws		#8, 3½"
Screws		#8, 1½"
Glue		

*Panels can be one piece or assembled from planks

PLAN

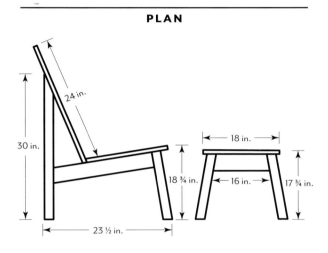

TOOLS

Tablesaw	Handheld drill
Measuring tape	Angled blocks
Pencil	Japanese backsaw
Clamps	Masking tape
Self-centering dowel jig or Domino	Random orbit sander

— 1 —

Make a full-size mockup. It's relatively quick and affordable if built from scrap. This is a worthwhile step to take if you want a chair that is actually comfortable. Modify it as needed until you are pleased with the design. When the mockup is complete, use it to take measurements and angles for the process going forward.

— 2 —

Mmmmm, flaky paint. Rip your reclaimed stock (shown here are old green-painted 2x6s) into 2"-wide strips for the front and rear legs. The bottoms are cut at an angle so they sit flat. Use your full-size mock drawing to determine the angle.

— 3 —

Cut out the front legs. To establish the angle and position of the cut at the top of the front legs, just mark it from the mockup. Again, quick and easy.

— 4 —

Create the leg joints. Beefy dowels and lots of glue create strong corner joints. A self-centering dowel jig like this is inexpensive and worth every penny. After drilling, use angled blocks to keep the clamping pressure even as you glue the joints. Assemble both sides of the chair.

— 5 —

Clamp up the stretchers. Connect the side assemblies with a horizontal stretcher. Use 3 ½" screws and piloted ⅜" holes.

— 6 —

Angle the back. Mark the angled cut on the back of the chair by setting a placeholder back into position and then use a spacer to transfer this angle back onto the side of the rear leg.

— 7 —

A handsaw helps. The angled cut at the back of the chair needs to be accurate, and using a Japanese backsaw allows you to make a nice, controlled cut. The guide block clamp helps, but it isn't absolutely necessary.

— 8 —

Glue up the seat and back. The seat and back of the chair are made from glued-up, solid-wood panels. If you have any interesting old lumber that you've been sitting on for a while, now's the time to use it. Then you can sit on it in a much more literal sense.

— 9 —

The stool follows suit. There are no surprises with the stool's construction. The stool is pretty similar to the chair, without the extended rear leg.

— 10 —

Different piece, same joinery. Use dowels on the joints at the stool's sides. Two dowels in each joint offer plenty of strength. Again, you could use a Domino joiner if you prefer.

— 11 —

Screw it together. Clamp the sides, then add the two stretchers and pull the assembly together with a clamp. Clamp them up like the chair. Use long 3 ½" screws to secure the sides to the stretchers.

— 12 —

A necessary step. Rough lumber looks great, but be wary of splinters where you don't want them. For that reason, be sure to sand the seat components carefully. The seat, back of the chair, and top of the stool are then all attached with screws from underneath.

WHITE BOOKCASE

I got lucky and scored a good quantity of old poplar barn siding. It was in great shape, with a lot of old white flaky paint—just the way I like it—and at ¾" thick, it was thicker than usual. I decided to make a bookcase out of it. I knew I'd need to supplement my bill of materials with some other stuff, but I wasn't too worried: I figured I'd just get out some white paint and blend in any other materials that weren't already a match. This strategy worked out just fine, with the results being just funky enough to be interesting.

TOOLS

Measuring tape

Miter saw

Tablesaw

Clamps

Pocket-hole jig

Handheld drill

Dado blade (optional)

Stepped dowel kit, such as Miller

Hammer

Square

Pencil

MATERIALS LIST

PART	QTY.	DIMENSIONS
Bookshelf		
Sides	2	52" x 10 ½" x ¾"
Top/ bottom panels	2	22" x 10 ½" x ¾"
Shelves	3	22" x 9 ½" x ¾"
Back panel	1	51 ¼" x 22 ¾" x ¼"
Base		
Legs	4	7" x 2" x 2"
Long stretchers	2	18" x 2" x ¾"
Short stretchers	2	6" x 2" x ¾"
Pocket screws		1 ½"
Glue		

PLAN

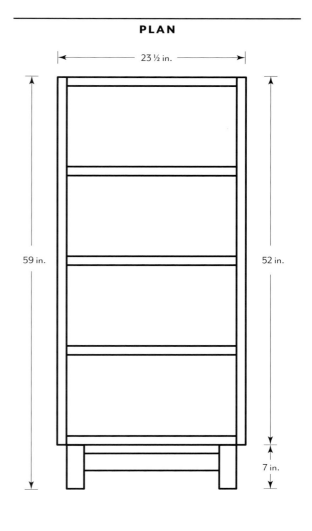

23 ½ in.

59 in.

52 in.

7 in.

— 1 —

Gather your materials. Unless you have some unusually wide boards, you'll most likely need to glue up panels to get the width you need. Start by cutting all the parts to length. Add a couple of inches so that you can trim the glued-up panels to precise length later.

— 2 —

Glue up the panels. Rip mating edges at the tablesaw or run them across the jointer. You won't need too many clamps if the joints are nice and tight. Just lay on the glue and apply clamps. Make sure the assembly stays flat by alternating clamps between the top and bottom of the panel.

— 3 —

Now build the base. While the glue dries on the panels, work on the base. It can be interesting to play with a few different shapes and styles for the feet, or you might just want to go with something simple and rectilinear, like these 2x2 oak corner posts joined together by horizontal strips of wood.

— 4 —

Good-old pocket screws. A pocket-hole jig makes quick and easy work of joining the sides to the legs; pocket screws are plenty strong for this job.

— 5 —

Spacing out. You could place the horizontal stretcher at the top of the base, but the space above it actually creates a bit more visual interest without being ostentatious. You'll also want to make sure that the most interesting parts of the wood face out.

— 6 —

Build the ends. To assemble the base, make sure to glue and clamp the parts firmly into position. Otherwise, they'll wiggle around and slip out of alignment.

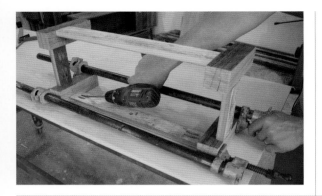

— 7 —

Add the long stretchers. Lay the assembly on its side to fight a bit less with gravity. And don't worry about aligning both long stretchers precisely. Just get one to line up where you want it and imagine that the other one is a acting as a spacer. You can fine tune the location after the first one has been secured.

— 8 —

Back to the bookcase itself. Cross-cut the parts any way you like. A tablesaw, a miter gauge, or a crosscut sled get the job done easily and accurately.

— 9 —

Groovy, baby. The bookcase sides, top, and bottom all need a ¼"-wide groove cut ⅜" deep near the back edge. A tablesaw equipped with a dado blade works great for this. No dado blade? Just take multiple passes with a single blade.

— 10 —

Assemble the case. To assemble the case, Miller Dowels are a great solution. These stepped dowels come in a variety of sizes and wood species. The inexpensive kits include a proprietary drill bit; all you have to do is drill the hole, add glue, and then whack the dowel into place.

— 11 —

Add the back. The ¼"-thick plywood back panel will slide into the groove near the back edge. Make sure to add glue to the groove, and mop up the squeeze-out while it's still fresh.

— 12 —

Bring it all together. Once the back is in place, stand the bookcase up on one side and add the other side. If needed, a few clamps can hold things in place temporarily while you work.

— 13 —

Keep it simple. While the clamps are still in place, position the shelves and drive the Miller dowels into place to secure them. Three dowels per shelf is just right.

COFFEE TABLE

One of the joys of working with reclaimed wood is savoring the range of interesting textures and colors you'll come across. This coffee table makes use of some nicely varied lumber for the top, and I took care to keep some of that character in the finished product. While it would be possible to plane the top down to achieve a uniform look after the boards have been glued up, this would miss the point, in my view. My process creates a panel that is not perfectly flat, but I don't see that as a flaw in this context. Any discrepancies can be feathered out with a palm sander, and this will allow the dings, scratches, and old milling marks to shine through.

PLAN

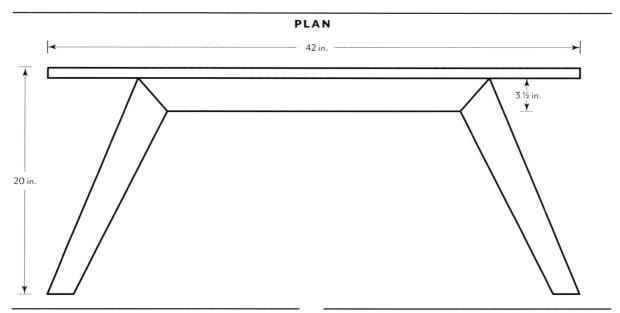

42 in.

3 ½ in.

20 in.

TOOLS

Measuring tape

Tablesaw

Clamps

Straightedge

Compass

Pencil

Square

Miter saw

Tapering jig for tablesaw, or bandsaw

Self-centering dowel jig or Domino

Handheld drill

Random orbit sander

Miter gauge or crosscut sled

MATERIALS LIST

PART	QTY.	DIMENSIONS
Top panel	1	42" x 24" x ⅞"
Leg blanks	4	22" x 3 ½" x 1 ½"
Long aprons	2	36" x 3 ½" x 1 ½"
Short aprons	2	17" x 3 ½" x 1 ½"
Glue		
Dowels		1" x ⅜"
Pocket screws		1 ½"
Braces	2	17" x 3" x ¾"

— 1 —

Play with the layout. Rearrange the boards that make up the top until you find an arrangement that suits your tastes. Once you're happy with the look, add glue to all the edge joints. After arranging the boards in an order that you like, edge-glue them together.

— 2 —

While the glue dries on the top, work on the base. As this design is somewhat bold, the large miter joint at the corners makes for some unique visual interest. Using a full-scale sketch makes it easy to figure out the dimensions and angles. For reference, the bottom of the leg measures 2" wide.

— 3 —

Sketching on plywood has its advantages. A template is easy to cut out and use for patterns. Wood patterns are less easily damaged than paper ones, making for more accurate and consistent work.

— 4 —

Trace the patterns. One long edge won't need to be cut, and one will.

— 5 —

Use the right tool for the job. Fire up the miter saw for the cuts on the ends.

— 6 —

Taper the legs. Cut the tapers however you like. You can use a tapering jig on your tablesaw to cut the inside faces of the legs, or your bandsaw.

— 7 —

Cut the long aprons. Use 2x4 stock and your other pattern to mark out the matching face of the joint. The side assemblies consist of two tapered legs and a long apron. This creates an interesting base that is both boxy, bold, and a little bit elegant.

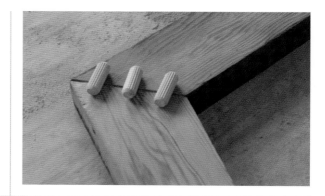

— 8 —

Plan your joinery. Use three beefy dowels in each joint. If you have access to a Domino joiner, that would be ideal, but this less expensive approach should work fine.

— 9 —

Not all doweling jigs are created equal. A self-centering jig ensures that the pieces will line up neatly when you put the dowels in.

— 10 —

Clamp up each sub-assembly. Run one clamp across the bottom, and one across the top. You can use small wedges at the top to prevent the clamp from marring the wood and to prevent slipping.

— 11 —

Join the two sides. The two sub-assemblies are connected by a pair of short aprons, also made of 2x4s. Set them in place with pocket screws. Placing the short stretchers across the miter joint should help to reinforce to the joint.

—— 12 ——

More is better. You'll also want to add a pair of braces at each end of the base that span from one apron to the other. This also provides an easy way to attach the top, as you can simply add a few screws from beneath the braces. Using elongated holes allows for wood movement to occur.

—— 13 ——

Smooth out the top. Once the glue dries, even out any overly rough spots. In this case, working around an old-school grade stamp was key—no way should that character be sanded off!

—— 14 ——

Cross-cut the top to size. Use a miter gauge or crosscut sled to cross-cut the top to its final length. Then simply attach it to the base with screws.

COUNTERTOP

Wood is a very traditional material for countertops, although it is most commonly seen in the form of butcher blocks. And while I love a good hard maple butcher block, and have made quite a few in the past, I thought it would be fun to experiment with an unusual approach using reclaimed wood planks. I think it came out great, and my clients did too. In terms of maintenance, there isn't too much to it. We sealed it with multiple coats of water-based polyurethane, which made it silky smooth, and we filled in big nooks and crannies to keep gunk from accumulating. And it isn't in an area that is likely to really see a lot of serious abuse, so I'm sure it'll hold up just fine. Worst-case scenario, it could always get another coat of poly in the future, although I don't see that as likely.

TOOLS

Measuring tape

Clamps

Track saw or circular saw
   with straightedge

Tablesaw

Miter saw

Nailgun with nails

Foam brush

Random orbit sander
   or sanding block

PLAN

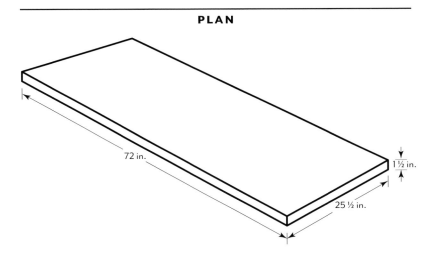

72 in.

25 ½ in.

1 ½ in.

MATERIALS LIST

PART	QTY.	DIMENSIONS
Top panel	1	72" x 25 ½" x ¾"
Long edges	2	72" x 1 ½" x ¾"
Short edge	1	25 ½" x 1 ½" x ¾"
Braces	3	23 ½" x 5" x ¾"
Glue		
Pan-head screws		as needed for attachment
Brown siliconized caulk or tinted epoxy		
Polyurethane finish		

— 1 —

Prep your stock. Prepare the edges of your stock and glue up a panel that is slightly larger than your finished top. To play it safe, it doesn't hurt to add 6" to the length and 1" or 2" to the width.

— 2 —

Miter the edges. Waterfall edges can create a thick look from thin stock. The trick is to cut long miters on the top and attach vertical pieces of the same material underneath. These long miters are best accomplished with a track saw, but you could also set up a circular saw and a straightedge. The process begins by mitering the front edge of the countertop.

— 3 —

Take a look. Here's a close-up of the cut edge. Take your time lining up the cuts—this will make aligning the parts a snap later on.

— 4 —

Two birds, one stone. This operation accomplishes cuts a miter on the edge on the countertop where a piece can be attached. It also frees up a piece of stock (the offcut) that can be mitered to become the piece that fits onto the newly mitered edge. The tricky part is that the offcut must be mitered again, but with the miter facing the opposite way. Even though it has a miter along its edge, the boards don't line up and "waterfall" over the edge. Use the tablesaw to cut the miter.

— 5 —

Repeat the process on the long sides. Hang onto the offcuts, because they'll be used as the edge pieces on the long sides.

— 6 —

Glue on the front edge. After mitering three sides of the top, you can attach the front edge— you'll need to miter it on the ends so that it can form a mitered corner with the long strips on the sides of the countertop.

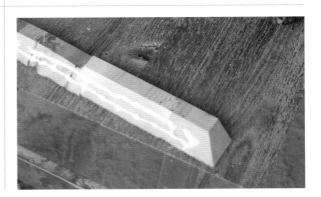

— 7 —

Why all the fuss? It may feel odd to cut long miters on parts and then turn around and re-cut them, but it really is the only way to achieve this seamless look. Totally worth it, right?

— 8 —

Create the long edge pieces. Once again, the offcuts will be have to be re-cut so that the miter faces the opposite way. Good thing you started with a panel that was slightly oversized, because a little wiggle room helps. Having the miters face the right direction will allow the offcuts to join up seamlessly with the countertop.

— 9 —

Miter the front edges of the strips. The fronts of the strips need mitered ends so that they can mate neatly with the piece at the front of the countertop. The two strips should be mirror images of each other; in other words, the miters on the front edges should face the opposite direction.

— 10 —

Assemble the puzzle. With a little glue and some nails, the parts fit nicely together.

— 11 —

Build up the countertop. To boost up the countertop and ensure that the edges don't hang down too low, add three braces to the underside. Don't use glue, because you don't want to interfere with wood movement across the panel, and make sure to pilot wide holes for the screws. This, in conjunction with using screws with large, washer-style heads, should allow for seasonal wood movement.

— 12 —

Reality-proof the top. Brown siliconized caulk or tinted epoxy is perfect for filling in any large recesses. In the end, these spots will blend it quite nicely.

— 13 —

Protect your hard work. Four coats of polyurethane, sanded in between coats, will seal the top right up. After drying, attach it to the counter using pan-head screws as required by the cabinet attachment points.

BOOKCASE WITH DOORS

This bookcase could be made in just about any style: if you were to use cherry or white oak, I think the design would feel like a refined piece of furniture that would be quite at home in a fairly traditional interior. In this case, though, I wanted to celebrate the funkiness of some old, reclaimed wood I found on the curb in our neighborhood. I actually love the peeling paint and mismatched wood tones.

TOOLS

Tablesaw

Measuring tape

Clamps

Pencil

Bandsaw

Nailgun and nails

Miter gauge or crosscut sled for tablesaw

Handheld drill

Planer

Hand plane

Self-centering dowel jig

Mallet

PLAN

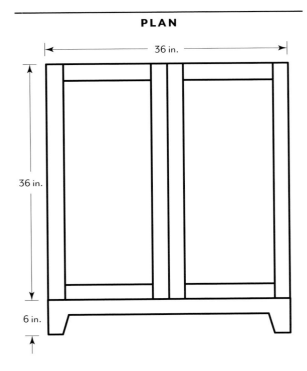

MATERIALS LIST

PART	QTY.	DIMENSIONS
Cabinet		
Sides	2	36" x 12" x ¾"
Top and bottom panels	2	34 ½" x 12" x ¾"
Back panel	1	35 ½" x 35" x ¼"
Shelves	2	34 ¼" x 11 ¼" x ¾"
Solid wood plugs		½" x ⅜" dia.
Doors		
Stiles	4	36" x 2 ½" x ¾"
Rails	4	13" x 2 ½" x ¾"
Dowels		½" x ⅜" dia.
Cup hinges	4	35mm
Glass (optional)	2	31 ½" x 8 ¾" x ⅛"
Base		
Front and back strips	2	36" x 6" x ¾"
Side strips	2	12" x 6" x ¾"
Joinery of choice		
Glue		

— 1 —

Begin with the panels. The bookcase is made of a set of four solid wood panels. Since glue needs time to dry, begin with the panels before you work on the base.

— 2 —

The corners of the base read as "feet." Just draw an angled profile that looks good to your eye, and then cut away the waste on the bandsaw. For reference, the feet taper from 3" to 2".

— 3 —

Build the base. Assemble the strips with glue and nails. The resulting base should be quite sturdy.

— 4 —

Size the panels. Once the glue has dried on the panels, cut them down to size. A miter gauge or crosscut sled on a tablesaw work great for this. Then cut a ¼"-wide groove near the back edge of each panel. This will provide a recess to receive the ¼" back panel.

— 5 —

Put the panels together. You can use any kind of joinery you like to connect the panels. There's nothing wrong with keeping it simple, like 2 ½" screws into countersunk ⅜"-diameter holes.

— 6 —

Progress you can see. It's nice to set the partially assembled carcase onto the base to get a feel for how it is shaping up.

— 7 —

Install the back. The ¼" plywood back should slide easily into the groove. This piece of ply was a little scruffy, which was actually just right for this bookcase.

— 8 —

Don't plane away all the character. For a project like this, a pass or two through the planer is often enough to even out the joints but still leave plenty of funky goodness.

— 9 —

The top and bottom are set in from the sides. The grooves at the back of the top panel are easily filled with solid wood plugs and shaved flush.

— 10 —

Adjustable shelves made easy. A shop-made drilling jig—a simple piece of plywood with guide-holes correctly spaced—helps create a consistent hole pattern on the sides.

— 11 —

Join the corners. Installing two dowels at the corner joints helps align the parts and offers plenty of strength.

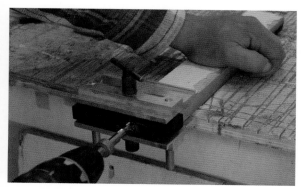

— 12 —

Test the fit. Before adding glue, dry-fit the corner joints to make sure everything lines up as it should. Once you're happy with the fit, add glue and clamp up the door frames. If you want glass in the doors, cut a rabbet around the back inside of the openings.

— 13 —

Cup hinges offer adjustability. Being able to adjust the fit of the hinges can be a plus when you're working with funky old wood and need some wiggle room to line things up just right.

— 14 —

Adjust as needed. Adjusting the hinges is easy—simply turn the adjustment screws to reposition the door location.

DESK

The lines of this desk are inspired by some of the Danish Modern furniture I love so much. The flare and taper of the legs create a striking design element that is repeated in the short legs that hold up the file cabinet.

MATERIALS LIST

PART	QTY.	DIMENSIONS
File cabinet		
Feet blanks	4	5" x 3" x ¾"
Drawer fronts	2	13 ½" x 10 ¾" x ¾"
Sides	2	24 ¼" x 17 ½" x ¾"
Top and bottoms	2	13 ¾" x 17 ½" x ¾"
Back	1	23 ½" x 18 ¼" x ¼"
Pocket screws		1 ½"
Screws		#8, 2"
Stretchers	2	13" x 2" x ¾"
Drawers (2)		
Sides	4	16" x 8 ½" x ½"
Front and back panels	4	12 ⅛" x 8 ½" x ½"
Bottoms	2	15 ½" x 12 ⅝" x ¼"
Leather	2	13 ½" x 2"
Copper brads	4	¾"
Soft-close undermount drawer slides	2 sets	22"
Desk		
Top	1	60" x 20 ½" x ¾"
Leg blanks	2	29 ¼" x 5" x ¾"
Leg connector	1	13" x 5" x ¾"
Pocket screws		1 ½"
Screws		#8, 1 ¼"
Water-based polyurethane		
Glue		

PLAN

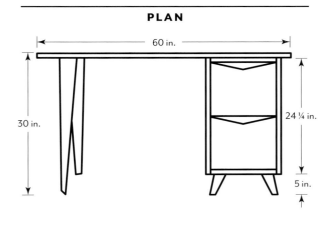

TOOLS

Tablesaw

Measuring tape

Pencil

Clamps

Glue

Circular saw and straightedge guide or tablesaw

Dado blade (optional)

Pocket screw jig

Handheld drill

Angle gauge

Nail gun with brad nails

Bandsaw

Jointer, belt sander, or hand plane

Miter gauge or sled for tablesaw

Scissors

Utility knife

Hacksaw

Belt sander

Foam brush

— 1 —

No need for biscuits. There's already plenty of surface area for a good, durable glue joint. A good fit between the boards is critical, as a proper glue-up shouldn't rely on pressure to squeeze together ill-fitting joints.

— 2 —

Clamp it up. If the joints fit neatly to begin with, simple panels like this shouldn't need a ton of clamps.

— 3 —

Assemble all the panels. You don't need to glue them all up at once. On the other hand, if you have enough clamps, it doesn't hurt to take care of the job in one go.

— 4 —

Trim the panels to size. Once the glue dries, use the tablesaw or a circular saw and straightedge guide to trim the panels to size.

— 5 —

Groove the back. The sides of the file cabinet need a groove on the insides to accommodate a back panel. Use a dado blade on a tablesaw, or a router table. You could also just make the cut in a couple of passes on the tablesaw, since there are only a few parts involved and swapping the dado blade in and out might actually take more time.

— 6 —

Drill for joinery. Pocket screw joinery is a good choice for assembling the case. Pilot the holes on the top and bottom of the cabinet.

— 7 —

Lay on the glue. A bead of glue serves as reinforcement for the pocket screw joinery. Keep a damp rag close by to mop up any squeeze-out.

— 8 —

Install the back. The back of the file cabinet should slide easily into the groove in the panels. Add some glue after test-fitting it. The glue prevents the cabinet from racking (wobbling from side to side).

— 9 —

Add the second side. Screwing the second side into place completes the basic structure of the file cabinet. Congratulations, you now have a box!

— 10 —

Create a template for the cabinet legs. It's fun to sketch out a few possibilities. When you're happy with the look, create a wooden template by cutting a scrap to shape. For reference, the feet taper from 3" to 2".

— 11 —

Patterns ensure consistency. After cutting and tracing four feet from ¾" stock that matches the cabinet, glue and screw them to the bottom of the cabinet. An angle gauge will help to consistently position the feet relative to the front (or back) edge of the cabinet.

— 12 —

Add some strength. To reinforce the feet (which would otherwise be rather flimsy), use an angle gauge with actual numbers on it to measure for a stretcher that connects the front and back feet.

— 13 —

Install the stretchers. The stretchers between the legs are installed with glue and long brad nails.

— 14 —

Start the long legs for the desk. As you did on the shorter legs, create a pattern for the long desk legs using scrap ¼" plywood. Aim for something with a pretty dramatic taper— to about 2" at the floor.

— 15 —

Draw out the legs. Trace the pattern on the stock and cut out the legs with the bandsaw. Clean up the profile with a jointer, although a belt sander or hand plane would be a good choice too.

— 16 —

Prepare the legs and stretcher. As with the short legs, the long legs are secured in place with an angled stretcher.

— 17 —

Create the leg assembly. Drill pocket holes in the stretcher and screw the legs to it. Once the glue dries between the parts, the assembly will be plenty strong.

— 18 —

Install the leg assembly. Position the legs on the underside of the desktop, then screw up through the stretcher into the desktop using four screws.

— 19 —

Create the drawer fronts. Remember that whole "gluing up panels" phase? You're not done with it yet. This time you need to glue up panels to make the two drawer fronts.

— 20 —

Trim the drawer fronts to fit. At the tablesaw, use a miter gauge to trim the drawer fronts to size. A sled would work as well. Test the fit against the carcase of the desk.

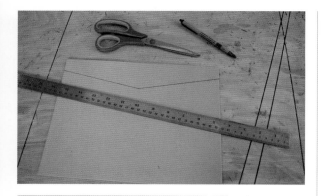

— 21 —

Create leather drawer pulls. The drawers deserve a special touch and leather creates a great contrast. These triangular shapes fit neatly on top of the drawer fronts.

— 22 —

Glue leather to wood. There's nothing tricky about attaching leather to wood. A bead of yellow glue works great for holding it in place.

— 23 —

Tack it in place. Reinforcing the glue with copper brads not only makes sure that they won't pull off, but also adds a nice decorative touch.

— 24 —

Cut off the waste. A utility knife quickly removes the excess leather, which is easier than worrying about aligning it perfectly at installation.

—— 25 ——

Ready the drawer stock. The drawers are made from ½" stock. You could use solid wood or plywood. The thickness matters; most soft-close, under-mount slides like these require ½"-thick stock, although some require ⅝". Make sure you're clear on which you'll be using before you proceed.

—— 26 ——

Assemble the drawers. The drawers are constructed in the same manner as the file cabinet—they're simply boxes with grooves at the back to receive a plywood panel.

—— 27 ——

Glue and brad nails are sufficient. Because these joints won't be subjected to a ton of torque, brad nails will work fine. You could use pocket screws, dovetails, or whatever drawer joinery you prefer.

— 28 —

Precision is key. To make sure that the drawers operate smoothly and line up properly, they need to be square. To check, simply measure the diagonals—if the diagonals are the same length, the drawer is square.

— 29 —

Prep for the drawer slides.
Modern soft-close undermount slides require a notch to be cut at the back for the runners to pass through. Consult the instructions of your slides to be sure of the dimensions required.

— 30 —

Attach the slides. Undermount drawer slides are easy to install. Just place them on the cabinet bottom and move them back 1" from the edge to allow for the inset drawer fronts.

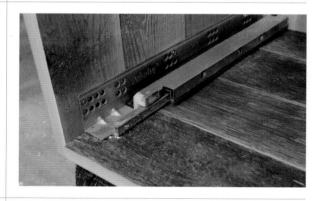

— 31 —

Mark the location for the holes. Start by setting the drawer into place and pushing it back as far as it will go.

— 32 —

A dot marks the spot. Upon removing the drawer, you can see small divots left by the hardware. In these locations, drill ⁵⁄₁₆" holes. There is one divot on each side. Manufacturers specify this location on their diagrams, but this method is quicker and easier.

— 33 —

Drill the drawer back. Once you drill the two holes (don't go all the way through!), the back of the drawer is prepped for installation.

— 34 —

Install clips on the drawer. These clip portions of the drawer slides mount to the underside of the drawer at the front. Attach them using four screws to secure them in place.

— 35 —

Install the drawer. Simply pull out the slides and place the drawer on them. Push the whole thing gently back until you hear a set of clicks. The clicks let you know that the slides have engaged with the clips at the front of the door.

— 36 —

Add the front. Attach the drawer front with a pair of screws from the inside. A set of clamps holds it in place while you work.

— 37 —

Install the second drawer just as the first. Set the height using a spacer block. Once the drawer is in place, the second drawer front goes on in the same way. Just pull out both drawers a few inches and set the upper front on top of the lower one, spaced ⅛" apart by a pair of shims. After adding a clamp or two, screw it into place.

— 38 —

Fine-tune the look. Use a belt sander to adjust the gap (aka "the reveal") between the carcase and the drawer sides.

— 39 —

Finish it off. Sand with 220 grit (you may want to skip the low grits, as they can eliminate a lot of the character) and then seal the whole thing with water-based polyurethane. After the finish dries, attach the cabinet to the desk top through the top of the cabinet with screws.

END TABLE

This handy little table is suitable for any number of applications, and its overall character varies quite a bit based on the material you use. While I often build furniture with grey and brown barnwood, I wanted something funkier for this piece, so I dug through my stockpile and found some boards with green and white paint to add to the mix. I built this table as a prototype for one I was planning to build in walnut, and that brings up another use for reclaimed wood projects—they're a pretty cost-effective way to try out design ideas you might hesitate to explore with more valuable lumber. In this case, I really liked the prototype, so the whole thing turned into kind of a two-for-one deal.

TOOLS

Tablesaw

Measuring tape

Pencil

Clamps

Jigsaw

Square

Bandsaw

Angle finder

Miter saw

Chisel or rasp

Self-centering dowel jig
   or Domino

Handheld drill

Wedges

Trammel

Belt sander

PLAN

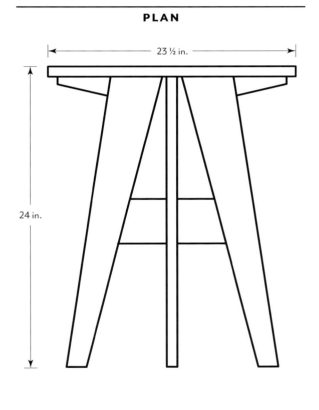

23 ½ in.

24 in.

MATERIALS LIST

PART	QTY.	DIMENSIONS
Top blank	1	23 ½" diameter x ¾"
Leg blanks	4	23 ¼" x 4" x ¾"
Top supports	4	4 ½" x 2 ½" x ¾"
Center stretchers	2	9" x 3 ½" x ¾"
Dowels		1 ½" x ⅜"
Glue		

— 1 —

Begin by gluing up the panels. This gives you a head start in the glue-drying department, so you are freed up to work on other things. For a tabletop like this, add a couple of extra inches to allow it to be trimmed to size later on.

— 2 —

Make a drawing. Not only does drawing out the shape on plywood make for a rigid drawing that can't get wrinkled or curl up, it can also be cut up into a set of patterns that will assist with production. A jigsaw is a great tool for the job. For reference, the legs taper from 4" to 2 ½".

— 3 —

Trace out the pattern. To create the legs, trace the patterns onto your stock. Line up a long, flat edge anytime you can so that you can save on the cutting and sanding. A jigsaw or bandsaw will make quick work of removing the waste material. To find the cutting angle for the edges of the aprons, use a simple angle finder. The magic number in this case is 11°.

— 4 —

Make the cuts. Set the miter saw to 11° and make the first cut. The second cut requires either flipping over the workpiece or swinging the blade to 11° on the other side.

— 5 —

Progress. Moving the apron nearer to the center of the assembly makes it more visible, makes the legs look less gangly, and it opens up a new possibility to how the table goes together.

— 6 —

Notches are the key. The concept behind the table is based around two identical subassemblies composed of legs and stretchers. The subassemblies are joined by notching the stretchers and placing them at right angles to each other. Use a bandsaw or jigsaw to cut the notches.

— 7 —

Make them tight, but not too tight. The notches in the center stretchers should require some hand pressure to go together, but not excess force. Also, they shouldn't fall apart on their own. When in doubt, work slowly and remove excess material with a chisel or rasp.

— 8 —

Simple joinery works fine. If you have a Domino joiner, by all means, bust it out to join the legs and stretchers, but that doesn't mean there isn't a good, less expensive option. While biscuits aren't as well suited to this particular application, long, stout dowels are a very good choice.

— 9 —

Wedges work wonders. To keep the clamp from slipping up the tapered legs, put a couple of wedges in. This creates a more even surface.

— 10 —

Is that top ready yet? Once the glue is dry, a makeshift trammel—created by screwing a length of wood to the stock—allows you to quickly lay out a circle.

— 11 —

Cut the circle. Use a jigsaw to rough out the top and clean up any inconsistencies with a belt sander. It shouldn't take long.

— 12 —

Add a few wings. Adding extensions to the top of the legs helps to support the top, and it also lends the table a more balanced look. For reference, these supports taper from 2 ½" to 1".

— 13 —

Attach the wings. Glue and dowels provide all the support the little extensions need.

SIDE CHAIR

I love chair making, largely because there are so many ways to go about it. The Danish Modern chair (page 30) presents a fairly refined process for building a more highbrow design, so I thought it would be fun to contrast that with a simpler, but no less fun approach to a chair I think might be at home as part of an outdoor dining set. The techniques are straightforward, and it won't take you long to build, but the process results in quite a sturdy chair nonetheless.

TOOLS

Bandsaw or tablesaw
  with tapering jig

Measuring tape

Pencil

Masking tape

Jointer or hand plane

Angle finder

Miter saw

Clamps

MATERIALS LIST

PART	QTY.	DIMENSIONS
Back legs	2	32" x 5" x 1¼"
Front legs	2	17" x 4" x 1¼"
Side stretchers	2	24" x 3 ½" x ¾"
Center supports	2	16" x 3" x 1 ½"
Back panel	1	22" x 8" x ¾"
Seat panel	1	22" x 17" x ¾"
Glue		
Screws		#8, 3"
Screws		#8, 1 ½"

PLAN

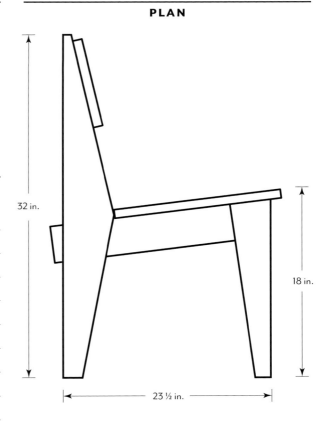

32 in.

18 in.

23 ½ in.

— 1 —

Cut legs to shape. Use the bandsaw to cut out the angled profile of the legs. A tablesaw equipped with a tapering jig would work as well. For reference, the back legs are 5" at the center and taper to 2" at the bottom and 1 ¼" at the top.

— 2 —

An unlikely design tool. Sometimes it's fine to make it up as you go along. Blue tape is a great tool to help lay out and think through the possible shapes, sizes, and positions of the various components.

— 3 —

A jointer comes in handy. It provides a fast and easy way to clean up the faces of your stock as needed, but a hand plane would work as well.

— 4 —

Cut the front legs. The front legs taper from 4" at the top to 2" at the bottom. Again, you can use a bandsaw or a tablesaw outfitted with a tapering jig.

— 5 —

Use actual parts as patterns. The front legs should come together easily enough. As with the rear legs, use the first front leg as a pattern for the second.

— 6 —

Set it in place. Play around with the placement of the stretcher. In this case, it is a playful design element because the stretcher extends past the rear leg of the chair.

— 7 —

Cutting flush on the front is important. Not cutting it here would just look like sloppy work.

— 8 —

Mark the top of the leg. The top of the front leg needs to be trimmed. Start by simply setting the stretcher in place and marking the overhang of the leg.

— 9 —

Determine the angle. Use an angle finder to ensure that you know what angle to use for the blade on your miter saw. Then trim away the offending portions as needed.

— 10 —

It's not exactly fine woodworking, but . . . Four sturdy screws at the joint keep this chair robust for a long time to come, and they're in character with the overall rough and ready aesthetic of the piece as a whole. Also, they won't be visible after assembly.

— 11 —

The first side becomes a pattern. Once one side has been assembled, it can be used as an alignment tool to put together the parts on the other side—this ensures that the two sides of the chair are consistent.

— 12 —

Clamp it up. The sides connect with a pair of stretchers than run beneath the seat. The one on the right is correctly placed—the one on the left is just wedged in temporarily and will be placed further back in due course. Trying to get both lined up perfectly from the get-go is an unnecessary frustration.

— 13 —

Secure it with screws. Long screws (3 ½") hold the sides to the stretchers. Make sure to sink them well so that the joint closes up completely.

— 14 —

Create the back and seat. Both the seat and back of the chair are panels of simple wood. Make sure to use a mix of painted and rough woods that work visually with the other components. Attach the back and seat with screws to the rear legs and the side stretchers, accordingly.

NIGHT STAND

Need a spot for a few books, a lamp, and maybe an eye mask? You bet. Why not incorporate a drawer for some extra storage? This fun little design offers practical features with the unique look of some reclaimed wood. I based the height off my own bed, so feel free to modify the dimensions to suit yourself. I also experimented a bit with the design of the base—you'll see a photo of this process—and I always suggest taking the time to do the same thing yourself. Who knows what you might come up with?

MATERIALS LIST

PART	QTY.	DIMENSIONS
Cabinet		
Sides	2	14" x 12" x ¾"
Top/bottom panels	2	22" x 12" x ¾"
Legs	4	9" x 2 ½" x ¾"
Front stretchers	2	16 ½" x 3 ½" x ¾"
Side stretchers	2	10 ½" x 3 ½" x ¾"
Pocket screws		1 ½"
Drawer		
Sides	2	9" x 11 ½" x ¾"
Front/back panels	2	22" x 11 ½" x ¾"
Bottom	1	21 ¼" x 9 ¾" x ¼"
Drawer front		
Panel	1	22" x 12 ½" x ¾"
Glue		
Polyurethane		

PLAN

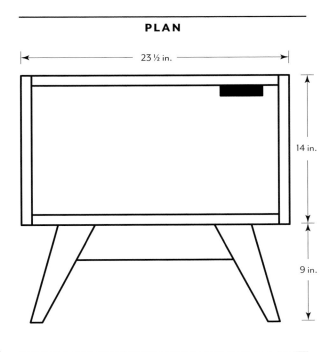

23 ½ in.

14 in.

9 in.

TOOLS

Tablesaw

Measuring tape

Pencil

Clamps

Bandsaw, jigsaw, or tablesaw with tapering jig

Angle finder

Pocket screw jig

Handheld drill

Foam brush

Jigsaw

Rat tail file or rasp

Stepped dowel kit, such as Miller

Hammer

Japanese backsaw

Random orbit sander or sanding block

— 1 —

Glue up the panels. This project requires solid wood panels glued up from smaller boards. A mix of painted and raw wood create a strong design element in the final piece. Choose your stock and glue up the panels required.

— 2 —

Square up the panels. Once the glue dries, rip the panels to their final width and crosscut them to length. To double check that the panels are square, measure their diagonals— the two measurements should be exactly the same.

— 3 —

Design as you go. Always be on the lookout for potential changes that might improve the look or feel of a piece. In this example, mocking up the "box" that is the heart of the nightstand using just clamps (no joinery at this stage of the game) helps to demonstrate whether its overall proportions are pleasing or not.

— 4 —

Feel free to experiment. With the box temporarily assembled, you can try out possibilities for the base. It often makes it easier to visualize how the whole thing might shape up. Straight legs were part of the original plan, but they were rejected in favor of something more dramatic.

— 5 —

Sketch until you're happy. It is worth drawing a few variations until you find one that speaks to you. The design shown here calls for simple legs that taper from 2 ½" to 1".

— 6 —

Cut the tapers. Either a bandsaw or a jigsaw can be used to cut the tapers on the legs. Of course, a tablesaw outfitted with a tapering jig would work as well.

— 7 —

Test the fit. Without moving the legs at all, the stretcher should drop neatly into place. Bingo.

Drill for pocket screws. Attach the legs to the stretcher using pocket screws. Begin by drilling pocket holes into the rear sides of the stretcher.

— 9 —

The front and back subassemblies are connected with horizontal stretchers. There's nothing fancy about them—use clamps to hold them in place, then secure them together with pocket screws.

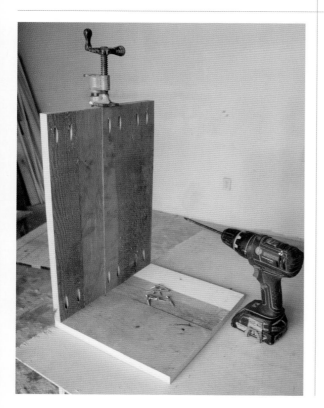

— 10 —

Assemble the box. Using pocket screws makes the joinery for this box simple. Remember to locate the screw holes on faces that won't be seen once the piece is complete—on the lower side of the both the top and bottom.

— 11 —

Complete the box. Clamps help position the parts as you drive the screws into place. Once all the pocket screws are installed and the nightstand is set upright, the holes for pocket screws won't be seen.

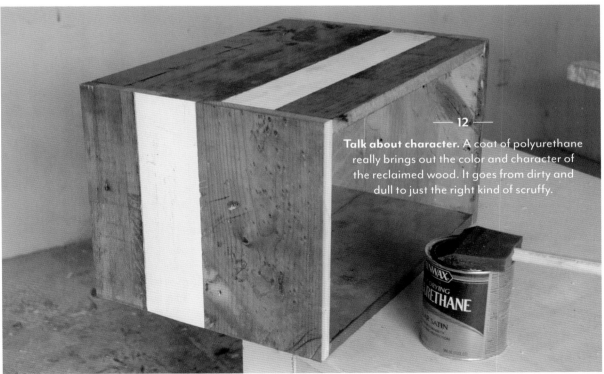

— 12 —

Talk about character. A coat of polyurethane really brings out the color and character of the reclaimed wood. It goes from dirty and dull to just the right kind of scruffy.

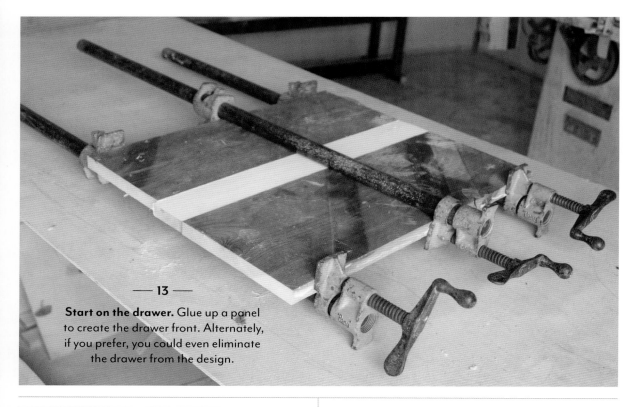

— 13 —

Start on the drawer. Glue up a panel to create the drawer front. Alternately, if you prefer, you could even eliminate the drawer from the design.

— 14 —

Cut the drawer pull. A cutout makes for an understated but interesting drawer pull. When the glue has dried, use a jigsaw to cut a notch. A rat tail file or rasp will clean up the cut as necessary.

— 15 —

Build another box. The drawer is a simple box with a ¼" plywood bottom that fits into a groove. You could get fancy and dovetail it together, or just use reinforced butt joints.

— 16 —

An easy solution. Miller Dowel kits come with a stepped drill bit and stepped dowels to match.

— 17 —

How do they work? Once the hole is drilled, simply add glue to the sides of the dowel and tap it home with a hammer.

— 18 —

A simple detail. Once sawn flush and smoothed, the dowel ends lend a nice decorative touch. Finish the drawer. Slide it into the cabinet and trim any tight spots on the drawer with a sander or handplane.

HEADBOARD

I've built a couple of versions of this headboard, one of which I've even gotten to keep for myself. It is a really satisfying project because, even though it goes together relatively quickly, it has a lot of what you might call "eye candy." Texture, contrast, pattern, movement—you name it, this project has it all. One of my secrets to keeping the process moving is to set the miter saw to 45° and then never move it; rather than resetting it for every other cut, I simply flip the workpiece upside down, as this produces a 45° angle with the opposite orientation. It saves a ton of time. I also let the strips "run wild" beyond the edges of the panel rather than trying to cut them all precisely. It is much faster to cut everything to size at the end in just a few cuts with a circular saw.

TOOLS

Measuring tape

Pencil

Tablesaw

Nailer with brad nails

Framing square

Jigsaw

Straightedge

Masking tape

Tracksaw or circular saw
    with edge guide

Handheld drill

Clamps

Miter saw

PLAN

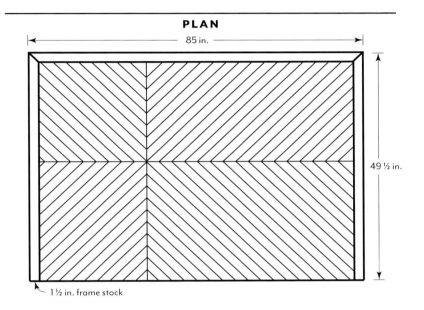

85 in.

49 ½ in.

1 ½ in. frame stock

MATERIALS LIST

PART	QTY.	DIMENSIONS
Plywood backer	1	82" x 48" x ½" (for a king; 62" for a queen)
Mixed reclaimed strips		Enough to cover 40 sq. ft.
Reinforcement top	1	82" x 1" x ¾"
Reinforcement sides	2	47" x 1" x ¾"
Frame sides	2	49 ½" x 3 ½" x 1 ½"
Frame top rail	1	85" x 3 ½" x 1 ½"
Screws		#8, 2 ½"
Glue		

— 1 —

Prepare the backing. ½" birch plywood is reasonably lightweight and thick enough for brads. Grade is less important than flatness. A single sheet makes the backing and a nice offcut. Cut the panel to size. Draw a vertical line 19" from the left-hand edge, and a horizontal one 30" from the bottom. These lines guide the layout of the strips. You could also center the lines for a symmetrical layout.

— 2 —

It's not an exact science. The precise proportions of the boxes created by the lines aren't critical; just space them so they look good to you.

— 3 —

Check and double-check. This project isn't particularly complex, but good work habits are critical because small alignment errors tend to multiply over time and cause real problems. You don't want that. To make sure you start with a square layout, make two marks on the top edge of the panel that are both 14" from the vertical line.

— 4 —

Time to rip some strips. This headboard is about 4' x 5', or 20 sq. ft. You need extra, but how much? Realistically, 40 sq. ft. is more like it, because miters produce more waste than square cuts, and even careful planning results in a certain amount of odd-sized cutoffs that can't be reused. Rip everything to 1 ½" wide. Keep the thickness between ½" to ⅝" (a little bit of variation creates some nice shadow lines).

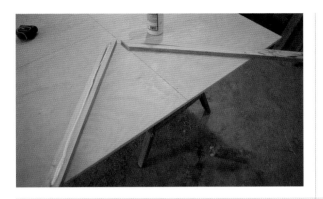

— 5 —

Line 'em up. After you miter the ends of the strips of wood with a miter saw, line up the first pair with the marks on the top of the headboard and glue them down one at a time. Use brad nails as well. If you have a reliable framing square, it doesn't hurt to double-check things.

— 6 —

Start square. Work slowly and check frequently for square alignment. The early stages definitely set the standard for the whole rest of the project.

— 7 —

Check as you go. Are your miters closing up tightly? That's another good sign. The second set of strips should be a perfect fit (they all should be!), which confirms that the strips are coming together at a 90° angle.

— 8 —

Momentum builds. Save time by cutting a miter on one end of each piece, then letting the overhanging portion "run wild." Put an imprecise mark (to the nearest inch or so) on the "waste" portion of the strip, then cut it. There are hundreds of cuts to make, so be precise where it counts and work fast and loose where it doesn't. By freeing up the "offcuts" now, you can press them into service right away.

— 9 —

Keep the strips aligned. Use a straightedge to branch out into a new area of the panel. This keeps the joints square, the lines straight, and the gaps (or lack thereof) uniform.

— 10 —

A pattern emerges. Getting the first couple of rows in is pretty gratifying. It's always nice to have confirmation that everything is lining up and you're on the right track.

— 11 —

Be a "big picture" thinker. It doesn't hurt to have a look at the next quadrant once you know that the left quadrant is shaping up fine.

Glue on the strips. Standard-issue wood glue does the trick. And don't be shy with it. Between the glue and the brad nails, these strips should be around for a long, long time.

— 13 —

A few hours later . . . progress! It is so satisfying to see this looking really crisp and clean. Small gaps may be unavoidable—it's reclaimed wood, after all—but the trick is to keep the strips properly aligned and the pattern preserved, even in the face of tiny gaps and irregularities.

— 14 —

Long strips are key. The right-hand quadrant is the largest by far. But it goes quickly if your strips are long and each one covers a lot of ground. Use blue tape to mark strips that are a bit thicker and require longer brads.

— 15 —

Time to trim the fat. Once the glue has dried, flip the panel over. A tracksaw is ideal for cutting off the overhanging strips; otherwise, a circular saw with an edge guide will work as well.

— A NOTE ON SANDING AND FINISHING —

Reclaimed wood usually has a bit of texture to it, and depending on the material you'll be using, this quality could vary quite a bit. Since a headboard will often see daily use, many people like to sand the texture back to the point where it isn't too thorny. This is a judgement call. My wife and I have been using ours for almost two years with nary a splinter, even though I didn't sand the wood at all. We prefer the way it looks unsanded, but you may wish to do a couple of small samples on scrap. When I build items like this for clients, I err on the side of caution and sand with 220-grit paper and then apply one coat of water-based polyurethane with a foam brush. This creates a very smooth-feeling surface while preserving most of the wood's character. It does darken the wood slightly, so again, making samples is a good idea.

— 16 —

It pays to think about the pattern. Personal taste and the materials you have on hand will dictate how uniform or varied the final result is. In any event, it always looks nice to have a few strips that "turn the corner" and continue a particular color or texture across a miter joint.

— 17 —

Add reinforcements. To give the frame something to be attached to, I attach reinforcement wood strips to the top and sides of the panel using glue and screws.

— 18 —

Now attach the frame itself. The addition of the strips to the plywood panel creates a very thick assembly —about 2 ½"—to attach the frame components.

— 19 —

Make and attach the frame. The frame is made from reclaimed 2x4 lumber, in this case parts from an old picnic table. The pieces are mitered and screwed into the reinforcing strips on the back of the headboard.

— 8 —

Glue up the panels. The project requires a top, a bottom, and two sides. Set out your boards and then edge-glue the joints to create the four panels. Leave everything a little long at glue-up, then use the tablesaw to trim them to size. Be sure to glue up panels for the door and divider as well.

— 9 —

Groove for the back. Use the tablesaw to cut a groove at the rear inside face of each panel. This groove will house the ¼"-thick back.

— 10 —

Give it a good look. Curious to see how the finished piece will look? A few clamps can secure everything in place so you can see where your project is headed.

— 11 —

Assemble the carcase. Begin assembling the cabinet. Apply glue at each corner and in the grooves used to house the rear panel. The rear panel helps strengthen the carcase, but also guarantees that glue-up goes together square.

— 12 —

Pilot drill for screws. The carcase is assembled using long screws. Before driving them home, drill ½"-deep ⅜"-diameter pilot holes so you can bury and cover the heads of the screws.

— 13 —

Install plugs. After putting 2 ½" screws into the holes, plug them using short lengths of ⅜" wooden dowels.

— 14 —

Sand them smooth. Once sanded flush and finished, the plugs lend visual interest to the corners of the cabinet.

— 15 —

Cut your divider to fit. Use a tablesaw
set up with a miter gauge to cross-cut
the divider panel to size.

— 16 —

Set the panel in place. Attach the divider
panel using pocket screws installed on the
inside face of the panel, where the holes
won't be all that visible.

— 17 —

Drill for the hinges. The cabinet door is just a simple wooden panel installed using 35mm adjustable hinges that are housed in 35mm recesses drilled on the door's inside face. The hinges provide plenty of adjustment—a benefit when working with reclaimed wood, as it can sometimes be a little bit wonky.

— 18 —

Install the hinges. The hinges recess into the pair of holes bored in the door. The other side (the mounting plates) are then screwed to the side panel of the cabinet.

— 19 —

Finish the rear panel. The plywood back of this cabinet is stained using a dark walnut stain to match the wood of the cabinet. Applied in a haphazard fashion, the finish makes the rear panel match the irregularities of the carcase.

BARNWOOD BAR WRAP

I am crazy about this project. My clients have a bonus room in their house that they have (wisely, in my view) redesigned as a bar. It is gorgeous in every detail. When I arrived, they just needed a finishing touch on the exterior of the bar itself. Topped with Carrera marble, it was ready for something really unique. The overall look and feel of the room is dark, moody, and glamorous, and I decided on a bold look to go along with the overall tone. By using reclaimed wood, we brought in a fun and interesting texture, and by weaving it across the front of the bar, we created a lot of movement and pattern. We were all pretty pleased with how it came out.

TOOLS

Measuring tape

Pencil

Tablesaw

Miter saw with stop

Nail gun with nails

Miter saw

PLAN

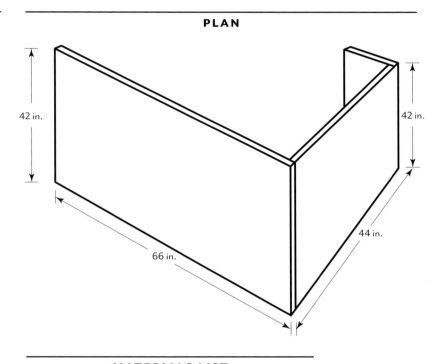

42 in.

42 in.

44 in.

66 in.

MATERIALS LIST

PART	QTY.	DIMENSIONS
Reclaimed wood strips	250	18" x 2" x ½" to ¾" thick
Construction adhesive		

*This project took around 250 strips and it covered about 40 sq. ft. When in doubt, make extras, as unusable offcuts will be created and eat into your stockpile.

— 1 —

Talk about a blank slate. Reclaimed wood—in a grey palette and a range of textures—are just the thing to dress up an otherwise plain bar.

— 2 —

Prepare the strips. Set the tablesaw fence at 2". This project required around 250 strips, and you'll want to cut about 20% extra, just in case.

— 3 —

A fixture guarantees consistency. Add a stop to your miter saw so that you can quickly and easily cut 18" strips.

— 4 —

The pattern is straightforward. Begin with one piece—the left one, in this case—then overlap its end with the strip on the right.

— 5 —

Planning ahead is key. Lay out a bunch of strips on your bench or the floor beforehand so that you can really get a feel for how it might all come together. This isn't a bad exercise to go through, and it moves along pretty quickly. When you're ready to weave in the next "column" of pieces (vertically speaking) you just follow the same pattern.

— 6 —

The money is in the corners. Filling in the middle of the pattern is easy, but wherever the strips hit the floor, a wall, or a corner, start measuring and cutting. If you imagine the bottom edge of the bench as the bottom of the wrap, that's where pieces will need to be cut to fit. More on this later.

— 7 —

Mix it up. The way you lay out the colors and textures is, of course, a key part of the process. It should look random but harmonious.

— 8 —

Stay organized. Make stacks of strips
and set them aside so that you can easily
keep count of how many you have.

— 9 —

Begin with the front. The front is the focal
point and utilizes the most full-length strips.
That way, the work goes quickly, and you are
less likely to have irregular or short pieces
in a highly visible spot. Begin by cutting a
compound miter on what will become the tops
of a pair of strips, and a regular miter at
what will become their bottoms.

— 10 —

The starter course is the trickiest.
Measure in a uniform distance (in this case,
9 ¾") from each side of the corner on both
sides of the wrap. I used 9 ¾" as the number,
but this was admittedly arbitrary. You basically
just need to know that the pieces you'll be
setting into place would be placed equidistant
from the corner, and with the lengths of my
starter strip, this was how it worked out.

— 11 —

Start slow. A careful start makes for nice,
even results later. With the compound miters
closed up, there is a symmetrical beginning
to the wrap on both sides of the corner.

— 12 —

Build on the starter course. Once the two starter strips are glued and nailed into place (use construction adhesive), set another pair on top of them. The length of the strips, along their bottom edge, is 2" less than the length of the top edge of the strip below it. If that sounds convoluted, look at it this way: each strip is 2" wide, and a strip needs to fit neatly at the bottom.

— 13 —

Pick up some speed. Once the starter strips (the ones with the compound miters) are in, positioning the regular strips is a piece a cake.

— 14 —

Create a clean look. Attention to detail and tight joints keep this project looking sharp.

— **CUTTING THE SHORT PIECES AT THE TRANSITIONS** —

This is the most time-consuming part, in my opinion, because the pieces have to be cut one at a time, and there may be some cutting and recutting in order to get things just right. It isn't that hard, at least: you just need to measure the long side of the piece that you need to cut, and use the miter saw to cut a miter on one end of the piece so that it fits neatly into place. You can then measure for the next one. And so on.

ROUGH & SMOOTH CREDENZA

I've long been a fan of Danish Modern furniture—it is my first love, in terms of design styles. I appreciate the juxtaposition of smooth curves, rakish angles, and flowing lines. I wanted to build a credenza that paid homage to Danish Modern without being a completely slavish imitation. Rather than using walnut or teak, as may have been typical for the period, I used Baltic birch plywood, and left the edges uncovered so the core shows through. I made the doors from reclaimed barnwood to create a striking visual and textural element, and also to play up a sense of contrast: old meets new. Finally, the simple iron pulls provide further contrast and a sense of rawness I thought matched both the birch case and the barnwood doors. The resulting piece is versatile in terms of its ability to blend into all kinds of spaces.

TOOLS

Measuring tape

Pencil

Tablesaw

Bandsaw or jigsaw

Oscillating spindle sander
or sanding drum

Self-centering dowel jig
or Domino

Clamps

Random orbit sander

Router with roundover bit

Tablesaw miter gauge
or miter saw

Dado blade (optional)

Handheld drill

MATERIALS LIST

PART	QTY.	DIMENSIONS
Cabinet		
Sides	2	29 ¼" x 18" x ¾"
Bottom	1	58 ½" x 18" x ¾"
Top	1	62" x 18" x ¾"
Back panel	1	59" x 29" x ¼"
Doors	2	29 ¼" x 29 ⅛" x ¾"
Cross-pieces	4	27 ½" x 1 ½" x ¾"
Cup hinges	4	35mm
Base		
Feet	4	6" x 4" x ¾"
Long rails	2	48" x 2 ½" x ¾"
Short rails	2	14 ½" x 2 ½" x ¾"
Glue		

PLAN

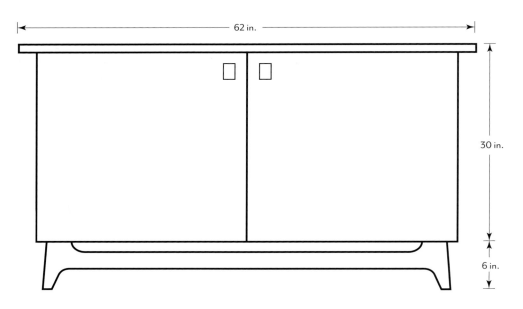

62 in.

30 in.

6 in.

— 1 —

Start with the base. To build the base, start with strips of ¾" Baltic birch. If you have any scraps around, this is a great way to use them up.

— 2 —

Make some blanks for the feet. Rip a 6"-wide piece of ¾" Baltic birch so that you have material ready for the feet. Then place the foot on the end of the blank and trace the pattern. For reference, the top of this pattern is 4" wide and the bottom is 2".

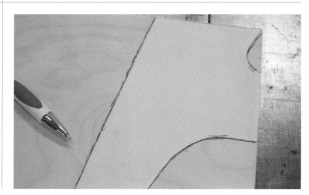

— 3 —

Start cutting out the feet. Use a bandsaw or jigsaw, but the tablesaw is faster and provides a cleaner cut. Set the miter gauge to 5° and cross-cut the blank along the line at the edge of the foot. After each cut, trace the pattern onto the freshly cut end of the blank. By resetting the miter gauge to zero, you create a foot with an edge perpendicular to the floor and one angled 5° from the floor.

— 4 —

Finish the feet. The bandsaw is the best way to remove the extra material from the feet, although a jigsaw with a sharp blade is a reasonable substitute.

— 5 —

Sand it smooth. Remove the saw marks with an oscillating spindle sander or a drill with a sanding drum. You can see how nicely the sanding drum fits into the concave curve on the foot; having a close fit like this makes it a bit easier to get a smooth, chatter-free result.

— 6 —

Cut the rails and join the feet. Connect the feet to the long rails at the front and back of the base using either the Domino (as seen here) or dowels. In either case, mark the centerlines of the joint on the face of the stock.

— 7 —

The Domino fits snugly in the mortises.
Apply glue inside the mortise, on the tenon, and on the ends of the rail and foot. Keep a damp cloth close by during glue up so that you can wipe off any squeeze-out immediately; once it has set, it'll be hard to remove.

— 8 —

Glue it up. Gluing up the long rails and feet isn't difficult, but it does take some precision. It helps to lay out the parts on long flat boards so the whole assembly ends up flat with no twists. Position a clamp at the top edge and the bottom, and slowly alternate clamps as you tighten them so that neither clamp gets too tight and pulls open the joint on the opposite side.

— 9 —

Once the glue is dry, use a sander to blend the joints between the feet and the rails.
Once they're perfectly flush, use a router with a roundover bit to ease the edges. It almost makes the rail and foot feel like they're made from one piece.

— 10 —

Connect the front and back with stretchers.
The short stretchers are just simple rectangles made from ¾" Baltic birch plywood. Use a miter gauge or a miter saw to cut them to length. Then clamp up the base. Use spacer blocks underneath the stretchers to keep them at the proper height. The base is shown upside down in the photo.

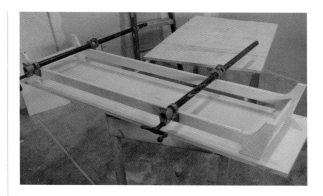

— 11 —

Switch focus to the cabinet. A tablesaw is a great tool for cutting out the parts, although a tracksaw is nifty if you have one. Cut out the sides, top, and bottom for the cabinet all at once. This helps to ensure that the parts are of consistent sizes (since you'll be working from one setup instead of a few), and it is faster.

— 12 —

A tablesaw is perfect for cutting grooves.
The back of the cabinet is made from a ¼" panel that sits in a groove on the inside edge of the cabinet parts. You can swap out your regular blade for a dado blade, but there aren't too many parts to cut, so it may be just as fast to simply make two or three cuts next to each other to add up to ¼"-wide groove.

— 13 —

Cabinet assembly is straightforward. Glue the side panels to the bottom panel and clamp them up. To secure the joint, use plugged screws, just like you did to attach the short rails to the front and back rails.

— 14 —

Things are shaping up. With both side panels attached to the bottom, you have a "U" shaped assembly ready for the back to be installed.

— 15 —

Install the back. The back should easily drop into the groove along the back. First test its fit, remove it, and add glue to the groove. This holds the back panel in place and keeps the cabinet from racking side to side.

— 16 —

Check the fit. The back panel should protrude ¼" above the top edge of the side panels. This allows the back panel to be inserted into the groove on the underside of the top.

— 17 —

Check out your work. The main assemblies are just about finished at this point. You could always use this as a jumping off point to make your own modifications by adding drawers, open shelving, or whatever design interests you.

— 18 —

Create the door panels. Cross-pieces on the edge-glued doors help to keep them flat—just elongate the screw holes in the cross-pieces so the screws can float from side to side, allowing for wood movement across the panels.

— 19 —

Install the hinges. 35mm cup hinges are a good bet when it comes to attaching the doors. They offer a lot of adjustment, which might come in handy if there is any warp in the barnwood doors.

— 18 —

Trace the triangle onto the blank. Cut it out with a bandsaw. A belt sander quickly cleans up any rough edges. Then use dowels to connect the parts.

— 19 —

Two clamps should be enough. If you set one clamp at each end, you can apply plenty of pressure to hold the triangle in place while the glue dries.

— 20 —

The opposite legs require a new approach. Cut a triangle in half and attach one half to each of the remaining legs. Use dowel joinery to make the connection.

— 21 —

The effect is nice and neat. In the end, this method makes it look as though all of the legs were attached in the same way.

— 22 —

Bring it together. For this leg, screw directly through the original triangle and into the half triangle. You're now three-quarters of the way there with the legs.

— 23 —

The final leg requires a new different strategy. You can connect the two pieces with pocket screws, and then plug the holes. With some sanding and a bit of stain, they'll blend right in.

— 24 —

To reinforce the whole base, add four triangular braces to the top. It's kind of a belt-and-suspenders approach, and it's a good idea.

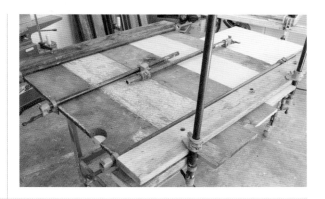

— 25 —

The top itself is simple, in spite of its size.
Gluing up a round tabletop is no different than
gluing up any panel. Just assemble the panel
and worry about cutting the circle after the
glue dries.

— 26 —

Let it dry. When the glue has dried, flip the top
over and use a quick, shopmade trammel to
draw a circle.

— 27 —

Quick and dirty. You can practice your
freehand jigsaw skills, but after you cut out the
circle, belt-sand any irregularities. Take your
time—it is a lot easier to go slowly and precisely
with the saw than removing lots of waste later
with the sander. Then simply attach the top to
the base with a few screws.

STATE SILHOUETTE

I've seen tons of this kind of thing on Instagram, Pinterest, and Etsy lately. And I have to admit, I'm kind of into it. Since my wife and I used to live in Wisconsin (Go Badgers!) and still visit once or twice a year, it seemed only natural to honor the state with a wooden cutout in its image. If you're looking for a quick and easy project, look no further. This will get the creative juices flowing and you'll end up with a cool finished product to boot.

TOOLS

Tablesaw

Clamps

Permanent marker

Bandsaw

Jigsaw

MATERIALS LIST

PART	QTY.	DIMENSIONS
Rectangular blank	1	24" x 18"*
Glue		
*Vary this as you see fit		

— 1 —

Choose a state. To begin, you'll need a reasonably accurate outline of the state that you have in mind. One easy way is to print one from online and then enlarge it on a copy machine. To make sure you have enough material, set the pattern on top of your strips of wood and make sure there is a little overhang on all sides.

— 2 —

Mix it up. As you layout the parts for the panel you'll glue up, play with a few different arrangements and decide what looks best to your eye.

— 3 —

Play up the textural contrasts. This close-up shows the awesome range of textures and colors you can use on your panel. That said, a more monochromatic look would work as well.

— 4 —

Lay on the glue. Due to the rustic character of the piece, you won't need to be overly concerned about making the end result perfectly flat or perfectly aligned. Just get a nice bead of glue on each strip and smoosh them into each other.

— 5 —

No need for excess clamps. Two on the bottom and one on the top should be fine for a small, straightforward assembly like this. Well-prepared joints require little pressure to close up.

— 6 —

Trace out the pattern. Use a permanent marker to make a solid, readily visible line around the pattern.

— 7 —

Cut it to shape. Bandsaws are great for quickly hogging away the waste, but you can't always reach the tight spots.

— 8 —

Jigsaws excel at detail work. With the right blade, they're a great tool for tackling the whole thing. Feel free to do whatever amount of edge sanding you prefer. As far as finishing the surface, the natural look is nice, or you can apply varnish.

Publisher: Paul McGahren
Editorial Director: Matthew Teague
Copy Editor: Kerri Grzybicki
Cover Design: Lindsay Hess
Layout and Illustration: Jodie Delohery

Spring House Press
P.O. Box 239
Whites Creek, TN 37189
ISBN: 978-1-940611-54-9

Library of Congress Control Number: 2018945888

Printed in the United States of America

10 9 8 7 6 5 4 3 2 1

Note: The following list contains names used in *The Reclaimed Woodworker* that may be registered with the United States Copyright Office: Craiglist; Etsy; Festool (Domino); *Harry Potter;* Instagram; Miller Dowel Co.; Pinterest; University of Wisconsin–Madison (Badgers).

The information in this book is given in good faith; however, no warranty is given, nor are results guaranteed. Woodworking is inherently dangerous. Your safety is your responsibility. Neither Spring House Press nor the authors assume any responsibility for any injuries or accidents.

To learn more about Spring House Press books, or to find a retailer near you, email info@springhousepress.com or visit us at www.springhousepress.com.

ABOUT THE AUTHOR

Chris was born in upstate New York, where he lived out in the sticks. His childhood was spent in these beautiful yet challenging settings: roaming around in the haylofts of old barns was a treat; getting up to milk cows in the morning was not.

Chris then attended Vassar College, a well-known stronghold of smart, progressive people in the Hudson River Valley. A year-long exchange program in Lausanne, Switzerland provided the quintessential opportunity of a lifetime.

After college, Chris spent a couple of years teaching preschool. He loved it, but gradually sensed that it wasn't going to be his life's work. Wanting to be creative and work with his hands, he got a job as a carpenter for a home builder, which meant he spent most of his time carrying around heavy things so more experienced people didn't have to. While this was rife with disadvantage, it did get him hooked on the joy of making stuff: it was the gateway drug that got him into dabbling in woodworking on the side. Much to his surprise, he woke up one day with the exciting and terrifying realization that he yearned to do it full-time, despite the fact that it was a horrible idea because he was broke, inexperienced, and clueless. On the plus side, he was young and energetic. With $200 to his name, he traded his mountain bike for a tablesaw, located shop space, and proceeded to make every mistake in the book. The first couple of years were pure trial and error: 70-hour weeks where he might've cleared $100. But he kept going, and the tide began to turn.

Although Chris never wanted to leave Ithaca, New York, he ended up moving around the country in support of his wife's academic career. As is often the case, these unplanned life changes worked out far better than he could have imagined. A four-year stint in Madison, Wisconsin was lovely, and then an unexpected relocation to Salt Lake City, Utah turned out to be a great move. They have been in Salt Lake City for more than a decade and love it. Chris has a wonderful wife and a beautiful daughter, and gets to spend his working hours imagining and building. In his free time, he skis, mountain bikes, and plays fiddle and banjo with the Bueno Avenue Stringband.

INDEX

METRIC CONVERSIONS

In this book, lengths are given in inches and feet. If you want to convert those to metric measurements, please use the following formulas:

FRACTIONS TO DECIMALS

⅛ = .125

¼ = .25

½ = .5

⅝ = .625

¾ = .75

IMPERIAL TO METRIC CONVERSION

Multiply inches by 25.4 to get millimeters

Multiply inches by 2.54 to get centimeters

Multiply inches by .0254 to get meters

For example, if you wanted to convert 1 ⅛ inches to millimeters:

1.125 in. x 25.4mm = 28.575mm

And to convert 60 inches to meters:

60 in. x .0254m = 1.524m

MORE GREAT BOOKS *from*
SPRING HOUSE PRESS

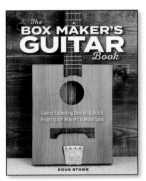

The Box Maker's Guitar Book
978-1-940611-64-8
$24.95 | 168 Pages

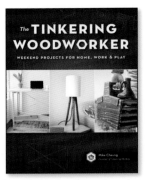

The Tinkering Woodworker
978-1-940611-08-2
$24.95 | 152 Pages

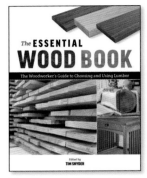

The Essential Wood Book
978-1-940611-37-2
$27.95 | 216 Pages

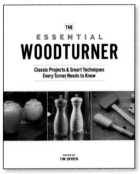

The Essential Woodturner
978-1-940611-47-1
$27.95 | 228 Pages

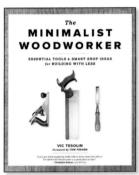

The Minimalist Woodworker
978-1-940611-35-8
$24.95 | 152 Pages

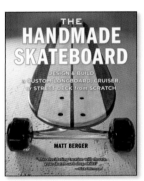

The Handmade Skateboard
978-1-940611-06-8
$24.95 | 160 Pages

Make Your Own Knife Handles
978-1-940611-53-2
$22.95 | 168 Pages

Make Your Own Cutting Boards
978-1-940611-45-7
$22.95 | 168 Pages

The New Bandsaw Box Book
978-1-940611-32-7
$19.95 | 120 Pages

SPRING HOUSE PRESS

Look for these Spring House Press titles at your favorite bookstore, specialty retailer, or visit *www.springhousepress.com*.
For more information about Spring House Press, call 1-717-569-5196 or email us at *info@springhousepress.com*.